The Adolescent with Developmental Co-ordination Disorder (DCD)

of related interest

Stephen Harris in Trouble
A Dyspraxic Drama in Several Clumsy Acts
Tim Nichol
ISBN 1 84310 134 3

Developmental Coordination Disorder
Hints and Tips for the Activities of Daily Living
Morven F. Ball
ISBN 1 84310 090 8

Freaks, Geeks and Asperger Syndrome
A User Guide to Adolescence
Luke Jackson
Foreword by Tony Attwood
ISBN 1 84310 098 3

Asperger Syndrome in Adolescence
Living with the Ups, the Downs and Things in Between
Edited by Liane Holliday Willey
Foreword by Luke Jackson
ISBN 1 84310 742 2

Haze
An Asperger Novel
Kathy Hoopmann
ISBN 1 84310 072 X

How to Help a Clumsy Child
Strategies for Young Children with Developmental Motor Concerns
Lisa A. Kurtz
ISBN 1 84310 754 6

The Adolescent with Developmental Co-ordination Disorder (DCD)

Amanda Kirby

Foreword by Professor David Sugden

Jessica Kingsley Publishers
London and New York

First published in the United Kingdom in 2004
by Jessica Kingsley Publishers Ltd
116 Pentonville Road
London N1 9JB, England
and
29 West 35th Street, 10th fl.
New York, NY 10001-2299, USA
www.jkp.com

Library of Congress Cataloging in Publication Data
A CIP catalog record for this book is available from the Library of Congress

British Library Cataloguing in Publication Data
A CIP catalogue record for this book is available from the British Library

ISBN 1 84310 178 5

Printed and Bound in Great Britain by
Athenaeum Press, Gateshead, Tyne and Wear

Contents

Acknowledgements

Writing a book takes time, and time with some people that I drive mad, and time away from others I should be spending time with. I have to thank both groups for surviving living with me.

Thanks to the team at The Dyscovery Centre, without their support there would not be a book in the first place.

Special thanks to Val who has tirelessly edited the book and sorted me out as well.

Thanks to my family and my long suffering husband and children, especially Andrew. Without his insight and understanding of his own challenges, I would not have written this at all.

Foreword

This book examines an area hitherto almost ignored by the literature: that of the adolescent with developmental co-ordination disorder (DCD). The last 20 years have witnessed a great increase not only in the amount of literature associated with DCD but also in the visibility and profile it has acquired in professional and popular arenas. It is now recognised as a developmental disorder alongside dyslexia, autistic spectrum disorder and attention deficit disorder. However, the vast majority of this attention has been paid to the age group roughly 5 to 12 years of age with little addressing the needs of the adolescent. The pubertal spurt occurs at around the time of adolescence and involves the child in great changes in their physical makeup, with anthropometric changes, together with the physiological developments modifying and significantly altering the child's capacity to perform skilled purposeful actions. Sometimes the increase in a child's strength at this time is a help to overcome a lack of skill, but at other times the changes in body resources are so profound that a child with difficulties may see these difficulties compounded. In addition, the social and emotional context into which the adolescent has now moved probably requires a different approach to intervention from that which had been previously employed when the child was younger. At a younger age, the child is more dependent on significant others to make decisions about his or her life; it is always advisable for the child to be involved in these decisions, but adults are often the 'choice presenters'. During and after adolescence, the young person is striving for more independence while wanting a security from which they can make their own decisions; consequently, any form of intervention must take this into account.

The most crucial contribution to intervention with adolescents with DCD is a recognition that it must be part of overall functional daily life and as such it must be in context. This book by Amanda Kirby from the Dyscovery Centre does just that. The recommendations are functional and the difficulties a young person faces are placed in the context of daily living. Thus there are chapters on 'Living Together as a Family', 'Social and Emotional Impact of Adolescence', 'Raising Self-esteem and Improving Social Skills', as well as suggestions for 'Strategies for Secondary School' and 'Transition'. Dr Kirby has a strong background that allows her to write with authority from a number of positions. As is often the case, her initial interest came about as a result of personal experience, which translated into the formation of the Dyscovery Centre. This establishment has, during the last five years, assessed and provided help, advice and guidance to several hundred young people with a range of developmental disabilities across the age range. Finally, Dr Kirby is well versed in the research literature and thus a book such as this is the essence of what has come to be described as 'evidence based practice'. The book is a welcome addition to the field, and will appeal and be of great benefit to parents, professionals and all who are interested in young persons who present a range of developmental disorders.

Professor David Sugden,
University of Leeds

Introduction

In the past few years there has been increased recognition of developmental co-ordination disorder (DCD) also known as dyspraxia, and other related specific learning difficulties such as dyslexia, ADHD (attention deficit hyperactivity disorder), and Asperger's Syndrome (a social and communication disorder). Until recently DCD was thought of as primarily a children's problem. The development of organisations such as Dyspraxia Foundation in the UK, and more recently DANDA (Development Adult Neurodiversity Association) along with increasing research in the area is an acknowledgement that some children will continue to have difficulties into adulthood. This is also true of other developmental disorders, that until recently were seen as children's problems that would eventually disappear. At the present time, the one thing that more often disappears is specialist services for the adolescent and young adult.

If you are reading this book, you are either likely to know an adolescent with dyspraxia or DCD or are teaching or working with children that may have some difficulties. You are probably aware of the problems to some extent. However for some children their difficulties may remain hidden into adulthood and present themselves as individuals with negative behaviour towards others, depressive symptoms or just feel that they are a failure rather than an individual that learns differently. One hundred years ago we knew very little about co-ordination difficulties and referred to individuals as clumsy and stupid, but in the 2000s with awareness and greater knowledge, we certainly should be trying to identify and support individuals through their learning years. We have a responsibility as parents and professionals to ensure that we provide learning in an environment that is conducive to all children not just a selected few. For some children, getting through the hurdle of school feels like climbing an icy mountain, slipping and falling on a regular basis but never quite making it to the top. The inclusive movement is working to provide education for all children but needs to recognise that different approaches may need to be sought for those with co-ordination disorders if we are to ensure integration and not further isolation.

At the present time the adolescent with co-ordination difficulties is often not able to access either assessment or intervention because of resource shortages. Support is often dependent on the basis of 'he who shouts loudest' and may be patchy and reliant on professionals who have a particular interest in the field of work.

Services in general are often delivered by a paediatrician, child and adolescent psychiatrist or occupational therapist up to early teen years but unfortunately often seem to stop abruptly with little handover to any adult services once the child reaches late teens and early twenties. This can lead to marked distress by parents and a void occurring while the young person struggles with his difficulties.

At this present time, there is no widespread routine screening of children undertaken to highlight those that may require additional support. Until this occurs, some children will pass into adolescence unidentified and remain 'hidden', perhaps presenting to others as difficult, lazy, poorly motivated, or withdrawn and come out of education with little to show for their years in school. The role of the interdisciplinary team, where health and educational professionals work with each other collaboratively sharing skills and information is still a long way from being standard policy in the provision of services for this group. However with shortages of allied health professionals, the only route forward to delivering help and support is to work collaboratively.

This book does not provide a simple or prescriptive route to success but suggests some ideas and considers where problems are likely to occur. The only similarity between one individual and another with DCD is that they are all different. Solutions come from talking to the individuals themselves and listening to what they want to achieve for themselves and to consider the barriers in place. Once this is understood the next stage is trying to find a route to success and the necessary steps required.

In general, 'he' has been used to refer to an individual with DCD through the book for consistency but also to acknowledge the greater number of individuals with DCD who are male. In areas where it is necessary to make specific reference to females, then this has been done. In general all strategies that can be used for the male are appropriate for the female as well. However the female with DCD may be late to present and not recognised, as the behaviour may present as being more withdrawn rather than having overt difficulties.

1 What is Developmental Co-ordination Disorder?

Success does not consist in never making mistakes but in never making the same one a second time.

George Bernard Shaw

Education is not the filling of a pail, but the lighting of a fire.

William Butler Yeats

Introduction

DCD is a common condition involving co-ordination difficulties that impact on living and learning. It is present in about 5–7 per cent of school-aged children. In the UK it is often referred to as dyspraxia.

Research has shown that the prevalence may be even higher than was previously believed. Kadesjo and Gillberg (1998) examined all seven-year-old children in one city in Sweden and found that 7.3 per cent had moderate to severe DCD with a boy:girl ratio of 5.3:1.

The most typical difficulties identified by parents of young children are with the following: dressing, eating, doing activities under time pressure, and riding a bike. In the school setting, the most typical problems mentioned include: writing, using scissors, puzzle activities, changing for P.E., ball skills, and running. DCD affects activities both at school and at home. In primary school, actions such as constructing, writing, drawing, playing are part of everyday functioning; while in secondary school, fast recording of information, keyboard skills and team games are part of everyday life. At home, self-help skills are essential to gain independence. Motor skills are a part of everyday activity. The child may have difficulties from the time he gets up till he goes to bed. Many children by the age of six years have gained insight into these difficulties and feel frustrated at their inability to do tasks that others take for granted. By the time the child makes a move to senior school, he is often feeling anxious about how he will adapt to new demands and may worry about starting again with a new set of teachers and pupils.

Overlapping difficulties

In considering the type of help required, we often label the child artificially and place him in a convenient box in order that services can be delivered. Children are all different, and where one 'learning difficulty' starts and the other ends is in reality usually blurred. It is important to recognise that the functional difficulties seen may commonly overlap for many different conditions.

As long as these functional difficulties are addressed and the individual can reach his or her full potential then it is less relevant what he or she has, rather than who he or she is and what he or she wants to become.

However, understanding why the individual has difficulties is important, in order to know how to help most appropriately.

DCD should not be considered as an isolated problem: there is substantial evidence of overlap with other disorders, such as dyslexia and ADHD (attention deficit hyperactivity disorder). As many as 55 per cent of those identified as having a reading disability (the term used for dyslexia in the USA) have also been noted to have motor difficulties, and in addition 32 per cent may also have ADHD (Kaplan *et al.* 1998). This combination causes difficulty for others to see clearly where the difficulties lie and what support is required. Studies have found that children with DCD display poorer social competency, have more academic and behavioural problems, and have lower self-esteem than their peers.

Gilger and Kaplan (2001) suggest that the very high overlap of developmental disorders is one indication that they are not independent. These authors propose the use of a new conceptual framework, which they called 'atypical brain development', to explain developmental disorders and their relationship to each other; one implication of this framework is that there would be a new emphasis on individual strengths and weaknesses of each child, with individualised treatment and support based on the child's profile rather than on a diagnostic category. The need for tailored support is essential, and profiling the individual rather than labelling is more likely to allow this to happen. This is echoed throughout this book by providing a menu of strategies, so that help can be specifically designed for the individual and made into a plan of action.

Into adolescence

Research suggests that DCD and ADHD in particular are not restricted to childhood. If the accurate assessments of needs are not undertaken and appropriate support not given, there may be implications in the longer term for these individuals (Losse *et al.* 1991).

In order to support the adolescent, the parent often feels like a mediator, communicator, therapist and counsellor, having to tell 'their child's' story over and over again to various professionals and other parents at different stages. This can be wearisome and can feel as if the only way to get help is to battle and negotiate.

The adolescent, by the time he reaches secondary school, may have accumulated a number of areas of difficulty. The transition to a new and larger school may end up being *the tipping point* as difficulties mount up and lead the adolescent towards being unable to cope. This is in contrast with primary school, where support may have been sufficient and the environment small. Furthermore, once the child moves into secondary school, close contact with the school may be more difficult to achieve. Waiting at the school gate happens less as more children take themselves to school. Popping into the classroom for a chat with Mrs Jones happens far less, and so close relationships between home and school are often harder to develop. There is a fine line for the parents to tread, knowing when to go and talk to the teacher about difficulties that are being witnessed at home and when the child should sort them out for himself.

Some individuals seem to benefit from their growth spurt during adolescence, and this may be caused by enhancement of maturation of parts of their central nervous system. However, others may find their co-ordination worsens during this time.

The child with more severe and complex difficulties is more likely to continue to have functional difficulties into adolescence and into adulthood. There is some evidence that individuals may also be more likely to be held back a year or to have been placed in lower sets. They may also be likely to have lower academic ambitions. This may be related to poorer self-concept. Children with additional attention and concentration difficulties as well as co-ordination difficulties, called 'deficit of attention, motor co-ordination and perception' (DAMP), have also been seen to have more behavioural problems in adolescence.

Becoming an adult

For individuals at the mild end of the DCD spectrum, the outcome into adulthood is usually good, as many individuals will often learn to compensate for their difficulties as long as their self-esteem has been maintained and they can see strengths rather than just difficulties. However 50 per cent of motor-impaired children will still have motor difficulties into adulthood.

DCD may affect the type of career choices the individual makes, as he perceives himself less able than he may actually be. Skinner and Piek

(2001) showed that individuals with DCD perceived themselves as less competent in several areas, and as having less social support than those with no difficulties. Lower self-worth and increased anxiety levels have been shown in the DCD adolescent. This may reflect the increased demands as they move towards independence. There is also some evidence that the adolescent is more anxious than the younger DCD child. Long-term anxiety may lead to an increased risk of depression and social withdrawal in adulthood.

Good history taking – gathering information to understand where difficulties arise – can be of great help. Parents are great observers of behaviour, and so are teachers who spend many hours with their pupils. As long as eyes are open to the signs and symptoms and are able to interpret what they mean, addressing the issues becomes much easier.

Diagnosing the adolescent

There are few standardised tools available that are reliable and standardised specifically for the adolescent age group. However, using standardised tests in isolation may not allow for a real understanding of the present difficulties; they should be used to confirm areas of difficulty rather than be relied upon on their own. A good history of past and present difficulties from several sources such as teacher, parent and the adolescent themselves allows for a greater understanding of where help and resources need to be targeted.

Diagnosis at present is usually made on the 'history' – what has happened to the child from infancy to the present – and considers the pattern of development. Ideally, in order to understand the needs of the adolescent, a holistic approach should be taken and information gathered from a number of sources including teachers and parents. Information needs to be gathered over time, to confirm the areas of difficulty that persist in day-to-day life, and how they impact on the individual in different settings, and to consider where trigger points may be happening.

The consequent plan of action to support the adolescent should be decided upon in partnership with the adolescent and his family, to ensure the child's perception of needs are met, as well as including a plan of how skills will be acquired.

There may be pressure from teaching professionals for education to be delivered along traditional lines, when for some individuals this may no longer meet their needs. School may perceive that it is important for the individual to pass examinations, the child himself may want more than anything to be socially accepted, for example to be able to play football with his peers. At this stage trying to implement any plan without the 'buy-in' from the individual is likely to lead to a low level of acceptance and success.

What are the key criteria?

The DSM-IV criteria for DCD (see box) were developed by the American Psychiatric Association and are widely used in the UK and elsewhere. They are not the only published criteria: the World Health Organization has published an alternative set (known as ICD-10). The difficulty in using diagnostic criteria such as these is that there are no precise cut-offs and the descriptors used are open to individual interpretation. This is one method of 'boxing up' individuals with DCD but does not look at causation at all.

In order to diagnose adolescents we need to consider what are the unique features that highlight the co-ordination difficulties. If we use the DSM-IV criteria as a guideline for this, in the adolescent, as with the child, it is 'impairment *significantly* interfering with academic achievement or activities of daily living' (author's emphasis) which is the most important to consider. We then need to highlight in this age group what they are likely to be.

DCD may be a diagnosis of place rather than person. One person may see that individual as being 'clumsy' and another may not. One sporty family may feel that the one child in the family that can't play football really stands out and has real problems, where another family who prefer to read and do more sedentary activities may not even notice any difficulties or see them as a problem. This difference in perception is important also in the context of school and work. Co-ordination difficulties are only a problem if they stop you doing something you want to do. At present there are no blood tests to confirm the diagnosis; as such, DCD is a collection of symptoms rather than a disease.

DMS – IV 315.4

Diagnostic criteria for Developmental Coordination Disorder (Dyspraxia)

A. Performance in daily activities that require motor coordination is substantially below that expected given the person's chronological age and measured intelligence. This may be manifested by marked delays in achieving motor milestones (e.g., walking, crawling, sitting), dropping things, "clumsiness," poor performance in sports, or poor handwriting.

B. The disturbance in Criterion A significantly interferes with academic achievement or activities of daily living.

C. The disturbance is not due to a general medical condition (e.g., cerebral palsy, hemiplegia, or muscular dystrophy) and does not meet criteria for a Pervasive Developmental Disorder.

D. If Mental Retardation is present, the motor difficulties are in excess of those usually associated with it.

© 2000 American Psychiatric Association.

Key DCD symptoms in adolescence

The key DCD symptoms in adolescence are difficulties with:

- self-help skills – shaving, teeth cleaning, food preparation
- recording skills at speed, such as in examination conditions, dictation
- team games, especially ball games such as football where conditions may vary
- organisation and planning, e.g. assignments, money management and travel
- time management, especially undergoing any tasks under time pressure, e.g. examinations
- spatial awareness, e.g. social distance such as too little eye contact, standing too close to others

- social and communication skills (secondary or associated with difficulties), e.g. making and maintaining friendships, awareness of social rules
- mathematics – especially in geometry.

Case study

Steven was six years of age when he first realised he was different from his peers. At 11 years all he wanted to do was play football, but he had already been excluded as the other boys laughed at him. He was always late getting to school lessons for P.E. or football as he found doing the laces on his boots really difficult and they would come open again as soon as he had done them up. He knew he couldn't ask the others for help at his age.

Moving to secondary school for Steven was causing him to have sleepless nights, as he had seen his older brother walking to school with his rucksack on his back with all his books and knowing exactly where to put them during the day. He just knew that times were going to get worse for him and he didn't know what to do. The good thing was, he could go to school with his brother and he had also been at the school previously for a play Robert was in at Christmas. Steven was also going to have to wear a tie in his new school and the Velcro shoes that had fitted so far were now too small as he had suddenly grown. More laces and things to tie every day.

Steven had always had co-ordination difficulties and found writing hard work. His teachers at school would say he was a 'fidgeter' as he could never sit still for more than five minutes. Everyone knew Steven in the small village school, but the move to the much larger school posed problems that many children with developmental co-ordination disorder face in their transition from childhood into adolescence and beyond.

His teachers prepared visits and a transfer package to ensure he had an Individual Education Plan in place before he started. This was reviewed with Steven's input on a regular basis and his parents also contributed. The Special Educational Needs Co-ordinator (SENCO) in the school happened also to have a son with co-ordination difficulties and had a particular interest in helping individuals with similar difficulties. Steven was involved with the planning from the start and was asked what was important for him at this time. He said that he was keen to improve his ball skills to play with the other children. He also wanted some help to organise his work and help with essay writing.

A plan was set up and a mentor system put in place with an older boy in the school. Steven is still having some difficulties today but he does know who to go and talk to. The teachers are aware why he struggles sometimes and will offer to go over information if he has missed things. The next step will be college. He wants to be a landscape gardener.

2 Supporting the Adolescent into Adulthood

Introduction

Approaches to helping the adolescent
    Changes in time
    'Getting through' the curriculum
    Teenagers!

A Sufi story from the Middle East – learning what you need for life and not for school alone

The boatman

A scholar asked a boatman to row him across the river. The journey was long and slow. The scholar was bored. 'Boatman,' he called out, 'let's have a conversation.' Suggesting a topic of special interest to himself, he asked, 'Have you ever studied phonetics or specific learning difficulties such as dyspraxia?'

'No,' said the boatman, 'I've no use for those tools.'

'Too bad,' said the scholar. 'You've wasted half your life. It's useful to know the rules.'

Later, as the rickety boat crashed into a rock in the middle of the river, the boatman turned to the scholar and said, 'Pardon my humble mind that to you must seem dim, but, wise man, tell me, have you ever learned to swim?'

'No,' said the scholar. 'I've never learned. I've immersed myself in thinking.'

'In that case,' said the boatman, 'you've wasted all your life. Alas, the boat is sinking.'

Introduction

The important stages from primary to secondary school and onto further or higher education and into the workplace are explored in this book. In order to understand how to support the adolescent, we need to think about all day-to-day activities and where difficulties may arise both at home and at school that may create a barrier for success. Once this is understood, implementing the practical solutions becomes much easier. There are few quick fixes, or miracle cures. As much as we would all like an easy, planned route to success, this rarely exists. However, if we can understand why the individual is having difficulties which are preventing him fully integrating into home and school life, solutions *can* be found.

Sometimes they may even seem relatively simple. However knowing where to start can be difficult, especially if a parent is so close to the child that the difficulties have crept up on the family. An external perspective can sometimes highlight where the problems lie and enable a strategy to be constructed.

Evidence-based approaches to helping the adolescent with DCD are still few and far between. Most research, assessment and intervention for children with DCD has so far focused on the primary school age child. There are now a number of motor programmes running in schools for this younger age group to improve motor co-ordination, and some are starting to drift into secondary school. However alternative sporting choices, apart from team sports where there is an opportunity to improve co-ordination, are often limited. Treatment programmes used by occupational therapists and physiotherapists are often directed towards younger children. This may be partly because of shortages of allied health professionals available to deliver support and may also be a lack of awareness of the longer-term implications of DCD and the range of difficulties that may occur at this age.

At present, young adolescent services are usually thin on the ground with few therapeutic approaches having been researched which address the adolescent's needs. Most parents work on a trial-and-error approach, feeling at times that error seems to be the more common path.

Approaches to helping the adolescent

The adolescent is often in a hurry to grow up and be independent. It no longer seems appropriate to do lengthy exercise programmes with the individual on a daily basis when there are larger issues to deal with. What are the priorities at this time? Are they about being socially able and having independent living skills in preparation for the next stage in life, or are they about catching and throwing a ball? We need to be realistic and appropriate at this stage and take a lead from the adolescent in what he sees as important to him. Often, as adults, our agenda can be different from the adolescent's. Encouraging movement through normalising activities such as swimming, walking, and so on, also encourages social skills for now and sets up a pattern of behaviour that can be continued throughout life. The aim of schooling should in an ideal world be to set the individual up for life and not just to get him through school!

Changes in time

In addressing the difficulties, it is important to acknowledge that as time passes, difficulties change. I am a parent of an adolescent with DCD, and have had first-hand day-to-day experience of living with a son with a living and learning difficulty as he grows up through the different stages of his life and the different situations that have affected him in a hundred and one ways.

I have also seen these difficulties change, and the ones that seemed so important become so trivial. Colouring in, an 'essential' skill when six years of age, becomes irrelevant at 16, when using a computer is of far greater importance. Learning to ride a bike, the skill he so wanted to acquire at seven is no longer of interest to him when the car in the drive sits there ready to race along the road potentially at high speed! Playing with friends takes on a whole new meaning when puberty strikes. Social ability is so much more important to gain when establishing relationships in the workplace looms in the near future.

Keeping the crucial skills for the future in focus is essential, if we are to encourage the children to become active and independent adults. This process cannot start too young, as it may take many years to gain confidence and to learn to adapt in a number of social settings.

'Getting through' the curriculum

Some of the difficulties seen with adolescents with DCD are because of the need to 'get through' the curriculum at a certain pace and the constant need to 'move on' to complete the curriculum. This pressure on the teacher means that it is harder to have different rates of teaching applied to different children who may take different amounts of time to learn. The child with specific difficulties is expected to learn at the same rate as the other children in the class. This may result in the adolescent having large gaps in his learning resulting in increasingly rocky foundations. For example, the adolescent may be able to tell the time, but may still have little understanding of time concepts and how they impact on his ability to complete a task, get to a class on time, or get to the end of an examination paper. Another example of this is where the child moves from primary to secondary school and has not acquired good ball skills, so that when faced with playing a game of football he has not got the skills to succeed, such as coping with direction, commands being called to him, and surface variations.

This inability to perform a range of tasks causes the adolescent to become increasingly anxious. This can result in social withdrawal or external signs such as emotional outbursts when others may least expect them.

It is important if needs are to be addressed appropriately that the adolescent is assessed to see at what level developmentally he is operating and to address the difficulties from both a developmental as well as functional perspective.

Help may be needed in areas that others would not expect such as wiping bottoms, cleaning teeth, eating neatly or even packing the correct books in the bag for school. Parents often express desperation, isolation and embarrassment that their child still cannot do what others would believe to be simple tasks taken for granted.

The child often seems at odds with his intellect. He seems able to understand the world around him but is not worldly. He is intellectually his age but his emotional and social responses are not in line with this. This incongruity is difficult for parents and teachers alike to cope with and may result in over-supporting or under-supporting, leaving the caring adult unsure when to apply pressure and when to pull back. The adolescent may vary in his abilities to do tasks, better in the morning than the afternoon, and even from day to day.

The child's transition from dependence to independence is a difficult one for all parents and not just those with children with DCD. Most of us want to protect our children and to minimise their traumas going towards adulthood. How much easier would it be to protect the child from the big bad world, but at the same time we all know that a tick in the 'independence' box shows that we have completed our role as a parent. The child with DCD often needs support more than others and for longer. It is a challenge to know when to hold on and when to let go. The child with DCD may be chronologically and physically a 14-year-old, while emotionally more like an 11-year-old. This is often not acknowledged in the classroom, where the amount and type of support the child requires to organise his work may not be recognised. At the same time, the individual may continue to need high-level emotional support at home. These difficulties may remain into early adulthood, and when others are fully-fledged independent learners the DCD adult may still need support and guidance.

The adolescent may have conflicting feelings of wanting independence like his peers while not having the internal strategies to be able to cope.

Teenagers!

Adolescence, for all teenagers, is a time of turbulence, but even more so for the individual with DCD, who is trying to cope with physical and psychological changes alongside difficulties that already exist in his life.

It is important not to assume skills are there even though adolescence has been reached. Puberty makes fast changes to the body and may make the individual seem more clumsy at this time. It may feel for the child that he is less stable and less able to undertake some skills he was competent at before. However, some of his difficulties may not be anything to do with DCD and may be just an angry and awkward teenager trying to assert his independence. It may be difficult to see which is the primary problem and which is the secondary one at this stage, as it all seems so entwined.

Most teenagers want to start to separate from their parents, and they become oppositional in a move towards creating their own persona. This opposition and trying to push the margins is normal. What is difficult to understand for many of us is when this is mixed in with the teenager who at times also needs support and emotional guidance and can appear still so young. Trying to assess which is 'normal' teenage turbulence and which are additional difficulties overlayed on top becomes a continuing challenge for most parents.

Case study

Tim is 17 years old and planning to go to college after he has finished his examinations.

Difficulties

He does not know where to start his work, and his room is in chaos at home. His parents feel frustrated shouting at him all the time, and he doesn't have any ideas what to do to make it better. His parents are worried what will happen when he gets to college and he has to tidy up and organise himself and his own work.

Solutions

Tim was taught some organisational strategies to help him.

- First a corkboard was placed in his room so he could put up his timetable to remind him when and where he needed to be.

- Baskets in his room were used so that clothes weren't scattered everywhere. He only now needed to throw his socks, pants, etc. into these rather than sorting them out.

- He was also taught to use a simple 'StickUp' computer program (see the example following) that allowed him to get his ideas down and then change them around and to create timetables for work to be completed. He also arranged to check with a tutor at school once a week for ten minutes so that he could go through what was expected of him that week and when work would need to be given in.

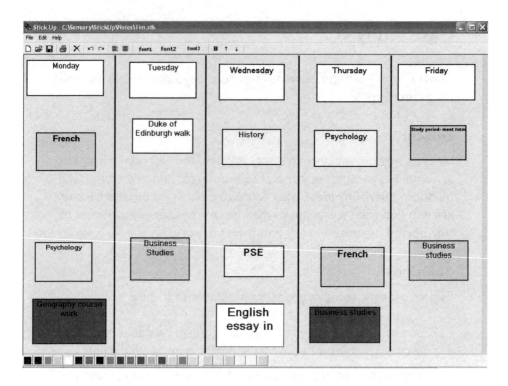

Figure 2.1 Sample StickUp timetable

3 How Does Puberty Affect the Adolescent with DCD?

Introduction

Periods, and self-care in girls
    Time concepts
    Fine motor tasks

New skill acquisition

Personal hygiene

Different perspectives – different outcomes?

Chapter 1

I walk down a street and there's a deep hole in the pavement. I fall in. It takes forever to get out. It's my fault.

Chapter 2

I walk down the same street. I fall in the hole again. It still takes a long time to get out. It's not my fault.

Chapter 3

I walk down the same street. I fall in the hole again. It's becoming a habit. It is my fault. I get out immediately.

Chapter 4

I walk down the same street and see the deep hole in the pavement. I walk around it.

Chapter 5

I walk down a different street.

Anon

Introduction

It is difficult for most of us to cope with the dramatic physical and emotional changes that go on through puberty. Most of us would not want to turn the clock back and go back and do it again I suspect.

For the individual with DCD, he or she may not really be ready to take on board the changes and may be emotionally at a level of a younger child, still desperately trying to get the foundation skills in place before moving up to the first floor.

This chapter looks at some of the subtle and not so subtle ways that puberty and DCD clash with one another. For many individuals, understanding who they are does not really come to them until their twenties. This has to be the most turbulent time and the time of greatest need for support by others.

It cannot, however be 'in your face', as the individual wants to gain a pride in himself and keep his already rocky self-esteem intact. This balance between help and guidance is one that parents have been trying to achieve for centuries.

Periods, and self-care in girls

Once a girl goes through puberty and starts her period, this heralds a time when she has to take responsibility for herself and become more organised. The school day means a big gap when mum is not around to prompt, and the teacher's role does not usually extend to telling girls to change pads at regular times for example. This can mean that disasters can occur if preparation is not undertaken. In order to cope, routines need to be created that allow a template for action, so this limits the possibility for failure.

Time concepts

Having an accurate concept of time is a problem for many individuals with DCD and this can affect girls trying to cope with their periods to begin with, for example in remembering and being aware when and how often to change sanitary wear and when their period might begin. A few girls may also not be quite as discreet as others in their disposal of pads, probably because of a level of immaturity and a lack of awareness of actions and their social impact. An inability to anticipate when periods start each month may result in the girl having embarrassing accidents while in school. At a time when street credibility is essential, this can further highlight the differences between the girl and her peers.

- If the girl is given a watch with pre-set timers to remind her to change her pads, this can help to cope with remembering this herself.

- Encourage the girl to change her pads or tampons at regular times, such as every break or lunch time so she can get into a routine.

- Spare pair of pants at the bottom of the school bag is always useful as a precaution.

- A calendar at home with days marked in and a prompt from mum will help to be prepared with pads, etc.

Fine motor tasks

The adolescent may have difficulty with fine motor tasks, especially when being undertaken without vision such as applying makeup, or using a lipstick or mascara.

- The young adolescent may benefit from having eye lashes dyed.

- A makeup lesson may also be useful to learn techniques that others take for granted.

- An easy-to-care-for hair style is also helpful.

- When shaving legs, an electric shaver is usually safer and easier to use.

- Consider using depilatory cream or have legs waxed as an alternative. Laser treatment now offers a life-long option for hair removal.

- Using lip-gloss instead of lipstick makes it less necessary to be accurate.

New skill acquisition

Young people with DCD are always going to have extra difficulties with learning new tasks that involve physical and organisational skills. With the right approaches, these difficulties can be overcome.

- Preparation and practice is the key to success.

- Create routines that become automatic – use visual reminders to begin with.

- Practise the skill in private – e.g. you may need to show the girl or boy how to shave – don't expect him or her to automatically understand what to do.

- Limit self-damage and increase success by using easy strategies.

- Be patient – learning a skill is one thing, remembering to use it may take longer!

Puberty brings for the boys an additional daily task of shaving. This may be difficult to achieve at first without some practice. Looking in a mirror and judging how hard to press and where to shave can be a real challenge and can result in cuts and lots of blood! Additional difficulties such as teeth cleaning may still remain a problem.

- Hair care should be minimised with a short easy-to-keep hairstyle.

- Use of electrical equipment such as an electric shaver with a safety guard will be easier, as will an electric toothbrush.

- Shaving foam helps to see where you have shaved and gives an indication of pressure required to remove the foam.

Personal hygiene

Toileting problems may have been present since childhood. Some adolescents still persist having difficulties cleaning after defecation. This may be because of instability, because of poor body awareness, or because of difficulties completing a sequence of tasks. This subject which seems so private is often not discussed among professionals or parents when trying to support the child but may be something that parents feel very frustrated about.

Difficulties with toileting can result in an adolescent who is 'smelly', and others end up avoiding him. Fear of going to the toilet in school may result in secondary associated problems, such as avoiding drinking to limit the need to go to the toilet, or becoming constipated, which exacerbates the problems. Some adolescents may become embarrassed and choose to hide soiled underwear so they don't have to confront the problem or their parents!

Useful information

- The wiping process needs to be practised, and the individual needs to be able to feel stable and able to hold onto something when trying to do so, such as a towel rail.

- Wet wipes can help the individual complete the task with greater ease, and they have a pleasant odour.

- The adolescent has to gain responsibility and should be encouraged to wash soiled underwear, or if this is not possible, at least to place it in a laundry basket rather than stuffed under the bed!

- Check the adolescent isn't constipated so that he can go to the toilet with relative ease.

- Establish a regular time for defecation, when he has time to wipe and is not in a rush because his mind is on other things or he is being shouted at from the front door.

- If you are encouraging the individual to clean his own toilet as well as himself, try using a stick-on product as opening a toilet cleaner with a safety cap on may be hard to do.

Case study

Lee was 16 years old when he started to need to shave occasionally. Looking in the mirror and shaving at the same time was pretty difficult. On several occasions he came down with only one side of his face shaved, apparently unaware of it. He learnt to shave using an electric shaver rather than a hand one, and got into the habit of feeling his skin once he had finished to make sure it was completely smooth. He would then check in the mirror for any gaps. His mother also offered her own input to prevent him going out half shaven.

Case study

Cathy, at 15 years of age, wanted to shave her legs. She did so, but put the blade on the wrong way and cut her legs to ribbons! After that she had her legs waxed by a beautician. She also found putting on mascara impossible, and also eye liner. On her 17th birthday her mother arranged for her to have a makeup lesson and to have her eye lashes dyed.

4 Living Together as a Family

Team work

A farmer who had a quarrelsome family called his sons and told them to lay a bunch of sticks before him. Then, after laying the sticks parallel to one another and binding them, he challenged his sons, one after one, to pick up the bundle and break it. They all tried, but in vain. Then, untying the bundle, he gave them the sticks to break one by one. This they did with the greatest ease. Then said the father: 'Thus, my sons, as long as you remain united, you are match for anything, but differ and separate, and you are undone'.

Aesop (650–560 BC)

Introduction

The adolescent with DCD will go through the same changes and challenges that his peers are trying to come to terms with, but will have additional difficulties to cope with. He may also have other overlapping learning difficulties that will impact on his ability to go through adolescence and on to adulthood smoothly, such as concentrating on tasks to be completed and socialising competently. Parents often bear the brunt of these adolescent stresses and strains. For the parent knowing when and how hard to push and when to support is a constant challenge. There is a need to gain independence; however, the need for continued emotional support may be as essential in maintaining a positive attitude and preserving the child's self-esteem. It is a fine balance for the parent to know when to be on the sidelines hovering in case they need to jump in and retrieve the situation and when to let go and allow the adolescent to learn from his errors. Social mistakes for all of us are a method of learning how to behave, but too many failing situations can leave the adolescent feeling too raw to even try again. Other adolescents will be interchanging quick-fire repartee and it is often difficult for the adolescent with DCD to keep up and exchange ideas at the same speed.

Home may become the safe haven when school becomes a day-to-day source of anxiety. It may seem that there is increased dependency on home at a time when other teenagers are trying to flee the nest as quickly as possible. Home may be the only place where there is constancy and stability for the child and where he feels truly respected and seen as himself and not as a set of difficulties. The problem with this is that the adolescent may want to be independent and be frustrated by his lack of skills and target his anger towards his parents who are trying to cope with his ambivalent behaviour.

Case study

'Better to light the candle than curse the darkness'

Sam was 17 years of age and his sister was 15 years. She was tall and attractive and glided through school, good at her academic studies and in the school hockey team. Sam came from a family where both his parents had successful jobs, and there was an expectation that the children would go to university and gain a qualification and go out into the world as able individuals in whatever job they chose. Sam was a worrier. He had always had difficulties at school and found team games impossible. From an early age he had known that he was different from the other children. He was now studying in a college of further education and was struggling to complete some of the assignments set.

He disclosed one evening how he was worried for his future. He could see his sister being successful and independent, and he still needed a great deal of support from his parents. He could not see himself being able to live on his own and support himself. He wished he could be more like his sister, who had loads of friends and a social life, and not find everything so hard to do. He told his mum that he could not see that he was any good at anything and would be unemployed and living at home for the rest of his life.

He said, 'I am an able person in an unable body.'

Sam wanted to talk about this to his mother, so that she might acknowledge that his feelings and concerns were real.

Sam needed to change some of his thinking and to see ways forward that would reframe his picture of himself positively. He needed to recognise the steps and route for him to be successful, and that the path may be different from his sister but no less valid and acceptable to his parents.

Support needs to be gradually withdrawn, and at a pace which the adolescent can accept. However, moving forward needs to be the aim rather than staying in the comfort zone. There are no easy solutions, and every family needs to accept that it will be trial and error and that it won't always go according to plan. That is a 'normal' experience for all of us. If skill acquisition is a goal, this can become an easier route – such as learning to drive a car, make a snack, go shopping, use public transport. These can be measured.

Family interaction

There are a number of scenarios that can have an effect on the younger person and his family.

- A younger sibling may already be more socially adept and able to undertake a range of independent living skills – this can highlight the differences within a family. The younger may be more socially adept, or have greater sporting skills, have some successes in school – all serving to highlight the disparity.

  This widens the gap between siblings and the individual with learning difficulties and he becomes more aware of his differences and difficulties. The younger sibling may even start to help the individual with his work and take on a 'caring' role.

- A close relationship with the sibling becomes stretched as he or she develops his or her own social life.

- The sibling without the difficulties feels guilty and wants to give support to his or her sibling but at the same time wants to extend his or her boundaries and seems embarrassed to bring home friends.

- The sibling feels frustrated at her or his brother or sister and the lack of skills in some areas.

A place in the family

The interplay within a family can cause stresses and strains for the individual, the parents and the siblings, and can result in a range of feelings that are not always expressed. Resentment can build up, and frustration can turn into anger. But sibling rivalry, as well as siblings being protective towards the individual with DCD, is normal. It is important to talk about the needs of the siblings too, and see that they should have protected time as well. Laugh *with* – not *at* – so that the adolescent with DCD can see the positives about being a warm and kind individual. Highlight and discuss the weaknesses and strengths of the whole family in a positive way, so that he can see that none of us is perfect and that we all have areas we would like to improve on.

As family dynamics change with the individual growing up, so do expectations change as well. Who helps in the house with what chores can be a common family debate. The child with DCD may be seen as less able and be allowed to be excluded from some chores and this can lead to increased resentment from other siblings. Being seen to be fair at the same time as ensuring that everyone takes a part is important if the adolescent is also to learn to become more independent and responsible for his actions. Otherwise DCD may begin to be used as an excuse for opting out.

It is important for families to acknowledge what seem to be simple statements but still need to be said.

- We are all different and each of us has value and a place in the family.

- Family activities should be encouraged, as well as individual activities. The adolescent already has a fragile persona – family time can be a safe place to practise skills that can be used outside the house.

- It is important for the individual with difficulties to have his own hobby that other siblings don't undertake as well, so that he can become 'the family expert' – e.g. photography, cookery, dog walker.

- It is important to acknowledge the sibling's feelings as real and allow him or her to have protected time with his or her own friends – the individual should not act as a junior minder!

- Fixed views of each family member should not be allowed to develop so that they can even become caricatures of themselves (e.g. 'Don't ask him to put the pictures up', 'She always burns the potatoes', 'He can't tell jokes').

Leaving home

It is hard enough for any young person to move away from home and to recognise how much support he will require. At times it may all seem an uphill task. Early and careful preparation will help to improve the chances of success and will attempt to predict where the 'hotspots' may occur.

Minimising difficulties has to be the aim of the game. We all have to take some risks and all of us have had to fail, pick ourselves up and move on. For the young adult who may have received more knocks, his ego may already be fragile and be less able and flexible to cope in these circumstances.

Any new situation can cause excitement as well as anxiety and it is trying to balance the two elements so that the individual does not become overwhelmed by all the changes occurring at once.

- Plan early if changes are to take place.

- Take a lead from the adolescent in order to understand his fears and tribulations.

- Allow him to try – be there to catch him if necessary – we all have to learn by experience and only practice will improve a skill, rather than avoidance.

- Prepare, prepare, prepare – consider the day from first thing in the morning till last thing at night – where could glitches occur and what could be done to minimise them? e.g. cleaning toilets in a flat (can he open a bottle?), using a kettle to make a cup of tea, washing hair and using a hairdryer.

- Make sure these skills have been practised beforehand – using a launderette or a washing machine, using an iron and putting up an ironing board, making a snack, opening a can, etc.

- Lead from behind, letting the adolescent guide the direction he wants to go in.

- Try to create a plan of action and divide this into short-, medium- and long-term goals, review the plan and alter it as necessary. This then creates a list of 'to dos'.

Moving to college

Before a move to college, it is important to consider what will increase the chances for success rather than failure. Being in a familiar setting such as your hometown can be helpful as the individual will know how to get around and what transport to use. He will also be familiar with local shops and may have a network of friends. A college or university near to home, so that he can come back easily if necessary, may also be a consideration. Moving too far away from the home setting is not always a great idea – if things go wrong the support structure is not in place or quickly and easily accessible.

If the individual is considering a new setting, then it is important that he has a head start getting to know the new environment. The first few days at college can be daunting enough anyway. Finding your way around a campus may be hard to do, as will getting to lectures on time, learning lecturers' names, and meeting new people. This sometimes leads to the individual 'holing' himself up in his room rather than being confronted by all the new challenges.

It also helps if there is someone the individual knows at the college as a starting point for friendships. This can at least act as a springboard. For some young people a new start heralds a new beginning after years of difficult times.

The following should be considered when choosing a college:

- Should this be in the home town or near enough to be able to get home?

- Is there good public transport?

- Is it better for the individual to be in a catered hall of residence to start with?

- Do you know anyone else there who could help springboard into a social setting?

- Are the college aware of difficulties?

- Have you applied for disability student allowance?

Case study

Emma was 13 years old and she wanted to play a musical instrument. She had tried the recorder and found it hard to get her fingers in the right place. She had tried the violin but had given that up after a few lessons. Her brother was great on the guitar and she did not want to compete with him. What she really wanted was to play the drums but thought she would just fail again.

Her parents decided that it would be great for Emma if she wanted to try playing the drums and arranged for lessons. The teacher knew there wasn't a rush, and that for Emma just to gain pleasure from the lessons was the key, rather than passing exams. She eventually got a second-hand set of drums.

When she was 15 years old she joined a band in school as none of the other kids played drums, and they needed a drummer. Her parents had also made another decision to let her brother learn the keyboard but NOT to play the drums, so it could be Emma's hobby alone within the family.

5 Social and Emotional Impact of Adolescence

Introduction

Peer relationships

Sexual relationships
> Practical implications
> Contraception

Behavioural presentations
> Practical strategies
> Understanding social use of language
> Negative behaviour
> Dealing with flash points

Strategies to minimise feelings of stress
> Advice not criticism
> Listen with open ears
> If you see resistance, don't push harder

Depression and low mood
> Poor self-concept

Negative narratives
> 'Life sentences'

While we are indifferent to our good qualities, we keep on deceiving ourselves in regard to our faults, until we come to look on them as virtues.

Heinrich Heine

From each according to his abilities, to each according to his needs.

Karl Marx

Introduction

The first attempts at relationships are hard enough for all of us, but even harder if the adolescent lacks confidence even in peer-to-peer relationships. Confidence required in sexual relationships requires a level of sophistication and an ability to pick up non-verbal cues and know when to approach or not to and how far to go.

The adolescent's self-concept and self-esteem are likely to be poor by this stage. He may see himself as a failure and not be aware of positive traits. The future may seem to hold only more of the past.

As other boys and girls are launching out into their social life around 15–16 years of age, the adolescent may still remain emotionally immature and unready to do this. He may be at a stage when he needs still to gain confidence in his own ability and should not be rushed into the next stage if he feels he is not ready. It is often the pressure by others that causes the most difficulties. The gap between the DCD adolescent (a boy especially) and his peers widens and may decrease the number of potential friendships when they were already thin on the ground. At this time he may start feeling depressed but not have the skills to overcome the difficulties.

- Learning social hierarchy and social distance are important skills to acquire.

- Learning new hobbies allows for an opportunity to meet friends and have a topic of conversation.

Peer relationships

Peer relationships in teen years are dependent on how you talk, what you wear and your likes and dislikes. However, the individual with DCD may not share hobbies or interests with his peers. In addition, the adolescent may not like to play sports. This leads to fewer opportunities to socialise. Lacking the opportunity to mix also makes it harder to learn the appropriate vocabulary and key slang words to join in. The individual needs to be aware of local colloquialisms or gestures; if he doesn't, this may serve to alienate him.

- The adolescent may require help in appreciating the need to gain an appropriate set of phrases and vocabulary to communicate with his peers. This may need to be through a buddy system or from siblings helping him as parents are often unaware of the terms and gestures used and their meaning.

- Use of text messaging or using the internet as well as face-to-face conversation may be a starting point for communication and be more comfortable and appropriate.

- Gaining a personal style is important. The adolescent may need to explore how he sees himself and how he would like others to see him. This help may be more useful given by an older sibling or young adult mentor who can see it from another perspective, rather than a parent who may think wearing certain styles of clothing is the right way to dress, but which sadly may be social suicide.

- The adolescent may be tempted to try alcohol or smoking to be like his peers. Alcohol may worsen his co-ordination skills, and make him less in control than normal. The very anxious teenager may see it as a way of relaxing and gaining confidence in new social situations and this may lead to increased dependency. This may certainly be true if there are associated symptoms and signs of ADHD.

Sexual relationships

In order to develop relationships with others there is usually a gradual process of making successful same and opposite sex friendships. Touch, hugs and eventually kisses lead on to closer relationships. The individual with DCD may have less experience even of the simple platonic relationships with the same sex, and may also have missed out from having non-sexual touch that usually happens playing team sports. Learning the whole process from scratch can be difficult for most, but even harder for someone lacking positive self-esteem.

Practical implications

Touch is an important part of any relationship. Some adolescents with DCD have been noted to be uncomfortable when someone touches them very lightly. If this is the case, then the individual may need to talk to their partner about their likes and dislikes and to share this before becoming relaxed in each other's company. Anxiety about being successful may also be linked to poor self-concept rather than directly related to the co-ordination difficulties.

Some adolescents with DCD are less of aware of the need to keep an acceptable distance when talking or sitting with someone, especially when the other person is not well known to them. Lacking awareness of this may result in these 'normal' boundaries being crossed too soon. This may also result in the individual coming too close and invading body space of others and be 'all or nothing' in his advances. Some may misinterpret this as being over-friendly, or it could even be perceived as threatening. Early on in a relationship, this may frighten off a girl, even though the intent was harmless.

The need to practise and be aware of the impact of non-verbal gestures on others is essential to prevent the adolescent not falling into a trap of a series of failed relationships. The individual may also say something inappropriate and lack the ability to repair the social situation. He may need to ask others why he made a mistake so as to learn from it for future occasions.

- The individual should remind himself to look into other people's eyes.

- Learning about posture using techniques such as the Alexander technique and Pilates can allow the individual to carry himself better and seem more confident.

Contraception

If the young adult is in a relationship and wants to consider having sexual relations with a partner, he or she needs to consider contraception. If the pill is considered, then poor time concepts may make it difficult to remember to take it regularly.

- A watch with an automatic buzzer or a mobile phone with an alarm can be used as a pill reminder.

- The depot injection lasting three months can be an alternative form of contraception if time management is poor.

If condoms are used, then fitting a condom may be more difficult if co-ordination isn't so good especially if the individual is in a rush!

- It can help if using a condom, to practise the technique rather than trying to use it for the first time when anxiety will be heightened and co-ordination may consequently deteriorate.

Behavioural presentations

The adolescent may display some or all of these behaviours:

- Grabbing someone to gain attention and not realising how hard or soft to do this.

- Hugging people who he may not know well, and not discriminating sufficiently between friends and acquaintances.

- Hugging mum or dad, or wanting to still hold hands, while out of the home – peers may see this and laugh at him. The individual may still lack insight into how this may impact on his attempts to make friends.

- Calling out too loudly, and not being able to recognise the need to modulate his voice.

- His voice sounding too loud or aggressive when excited and being misunderstood.

- Frustration presenting as aggression, especially when not being able to do a task and resulting in a 'temper tantrum'.

- Hooking on to disability rather than ability – and wanting to hold on to the DCD label 'I can't do that because I have DCD'.

- Not giving good eye contact or an appropriate handshake when talking to, or meeting someone.

- Making an inappropriate statement to someone, this being misinterpreted as rude.

Practical strategies

Social skills training can help the adolescent avoid some of these behaviours, but within a mixed skill group so that some positive modelling can take place. This can be difficult to achieve and may be best undertaken in a more naturalistic setting such as a youth club, rather than in a formal training setting.

- Understanding of social hierarchy – using pictures can help to both discuss and show examples of socially different behaviour.

- Use of audio and video can provide greater insight on how the adolescent appears to others – for example, he may not be aware of his tone of voice, or proximity to others. It may be necessary to point out what is inappropriate, as he may lack the knowledge and the strategies to change.

- Don't accuse – explain the problem.

- Allow the individual to talk through his day and highlight to you where he thinks circumstances may not have gone entirely smoothly – discuss with him alternatives for coping in this situation so he builds insight into where mistakes may have been made. This should be seen as a private session where this information will not be discussed with others so that he can feel safe to report what he feels has gone wrong.

- Give information – either orally or written, but keep it simple – you may be telling him to do a series of activities and he may not be able to hold on to the information. This may result in further confusion and guesses – sometimes being wrong and sometimes right.

Understanding social use of language

The adolescent may seem overly honest and say things that may be taken the wrong way. He may see things in a literal way and seem to be quite moralistic and tell others of his beliefs, even at the potential detriment of a relationship. 'He shouldn't do that – the teacher told us not to' may be right, but may result in the individual then being further alienated from his peer group. This shows sometimes as a lack of flexibility in interpretation of rules and over-rigidity in making sense of the world around him. This is in common with individuals with autistic spectrum disorders.

An awareness of differing social settings may result in the individual for example talking too loudly in church and not realising others can hear him.

- The appropriate rules for each setting may need to be formally taught and written down as a reminder and to build a social bible.

- A set of basic rules and additional variations on a theme may need to be created for each potential setting, e.g. mealtimes, conversation with different people, shopping, travelling, attending an interview.

- Modelling and practising different social settings prior to them occurring is important for the individual so that he has the skills and the confidence to cope once he is alone.

Negative behaviour

This may start to emerge when the teenager feels a lack of support from school and home and may feel the need to act out in a more obvious way his sense of distress. This is usually at a subconscious level. This may be seen both in school and at home, rather than just at home, which is the usual pattern for the younger child. The teenager with DCD may not have yet been identified as such in the secondary school and the presentation of negative behaviour may be the only outward indicator of his difficulties. Alarm bells should ring in school if a previously well-behaved child starts to change his pattern of behaviour. He may alternatively become the 'class clown' to gain recognition of any sort from his peers.

Dealing with flash points

'I've lost my locker key again' – the adolescent returns home upset and worried at the potential for getting into trouble when he returns to school. He reaches home and he gets told off by his parents for being so careless again.

Pre-empting a situation is often better than having to deal with the impact of the difficulties. If, for example, specialist and expensive equipment gets broken (say, a computer), this leads to huge amounts of friction between parent and child or between the child and school. Preparation for loss before it happens can minimise stress. Good insurance on any electrical equipment is always a good option, especially if this is going to be an important part of a survival kit.

Strategies to minimise feelings of stress

Seeing things from a positive perspective for the individual is essential at a time for many adolescents when they see life as an uphill struggle. It can be easy to criticise misdemeanors, rather than seeing patterns of repeated behaviour and learning from difficulties and seeing what support or changes need to be put in place.

Case study

Dealing with an incident

Jim was 14 years old and he had just been given a laptop computer to help with recording and organising information. It was quite bulky, and along with his other bags meant that he felt a bit like a pack horse all the time. In his school there were no lockers and Jim carried the laptop from class to class. One day Jim left his computer in the maths room as he ran off to get to P.E. on time. When he came back, it was still there but the screen was damaged. His parents screamed at him when he got home and said that he should have been more careful. 'How many times have I told you to look after your things – every time we buy you something to help you, you either lose it or break it.'

What has Jim gained by leaving behind his laptop? – He would not have 'done it on purpose'.
How else could his parents have approached Jim?
What could be done to help Jim in the future, to safeguard this from happening again?
Is a laptop the answer?
Could he have a locker?
Could he use a PDA or handheld PC?
Should all equipment be fully insured for breakages if it 'always' happens?

Advice not criticism

Using a lost locker key as an example, ask him how he may have lost his key, but don't criticise him and see it as a deliberate negative act but one that requires support and a strategy.

- Could you put the key on a key ring to attach to his bag or trousers to help him in future to prevent a repeat of the present situation?

- See this as a trigger or opportunity to look at organisational skills to help in other areas.

- Do you, if you are a parent need to speak to teachers and draw their attention to his disorganisation or does he not wish others to know? If he does, what will be the best way of approaching this – by letter, phone or directly? Discuss this with him, so that he is aware when you will be speaking to school so that he can be prepared for this. If you are in school, how could you liaise with parents so that he feels supported?

- Step back and look at why, and not what, the individual has done, especially if it is a repeat performance. Most of the time, repeated actions need additional support rather than admonishment.

- Allow the child to take responsibility once he has been supported with the necessary strategies to enable him to do so.

Listen with open ears

- He may not see that you are listening – let him know with nods and 'yes's'.

- Let him see that you are taking him seriously.

- Give him protected time away from other siblings.

- If in school, he may need protected time away from other pupils in a place of safety.

- If you hear yourself say 'Every time you do that…', ask yourself what could be changed. Repeated actions are often not the 'fault' of the individual and may not be able to be helped, e.g. spilling drinks or messy eating. – What is the individual gaining from these actions?

If you see resistance, don't push harder

- Ask 'Why now?'

- Have you seen this behaviour before, when was it, and was it over something similar – is there a pattern to the behaviour?

- If you push harder when he already feels pressured, he may have no option left but to lash out like a trapped animal with nowhere else to go.

- See what he sees are his barriers and acknowledge them as real. Ask him first if he wants help and then suggest strategies to get over them or around them.

- Tell him that you accept why he feels a certain way, but not HOW he is expressing it – but let him know how you would like it framed instead. He may not have an alternative way of dealing with a situation.

Depression and low mood

The teenager may show a pattern of poor sleep, variable appetite, poor concentration, and feelings of low self-worth. It is difficult to tell whether this is depression, as many 'average' teenagers will show symptoms that could be seen as depressive – teenagers often tend to sleep in, isolate themselves, are irritable and become non-communicative for years!

A girl presenting with depression may show social withdrawal and have even less interaction with her family or with teachers and may show additional difficulties, presenting with eating disturbances such as symptoms of anorexia or bulimia.

There is often a difficulty in identifying and separating out psychiatric illness from the normal range of teenage behaviours. This is one of the reasons that many individuals are not always diagnosed till much later and fail to receive appropriate treatment and support. Referral to the family practitioner or to a child and adolescent mental health team may be essential to ensure that adequate treatment and support is given if required.

Many adolescents may fall through service gaps and may find accessing appropriate services difficult as they don't quite fit into adult mental health services and don't fit into a learning disability service. Certainly after 16 years of age, this gap can widen as the individuals are no longer seen as children but are not quite adults. There is still a lack of training for adult psychiatrists in the field of neurodevelopmental disorders, and service shortages remain in this area.

Poor self-concept

The teenager is usually already weaker at sport, and as most games in schools are team-based it will mean there are fewer opportunities for the adolescent to have the teaching to allow him to gain sufficient skills to join in and enjoy any alternative sports. This usually leads to reluctance to try other sports and results in him or her being less fit and more prone to putting on weight.

There is some evidence to show that physically active students perceive physical education classes more favourably than less physically active students and that parental and peer support for physical activity influences the individual to increase their activity levels. The findings indicate that, by serving as models and supporters, significant others have an important impact in promoting physical activity in young adolescents.

Research with adults with ADHD has shown them to display a greater self-reported psychological maladjustment, more driving risks (speeding offences) and more frequent changes in employment. Significantly more ADHD adults had experienced a suspension of their driving licence, had performed poorly, quit or been fired from their job and had a history of poorer educational performance and more frequent school disciplinary actions against them than adults without ADHD. As we know there is a level of co-morbidity with DCD and ADHD in 50 per cent of individuals, so we can extrapolate that adolescents with DCD may also have a greater risk of this.

Certainly Gillberg and co-researchers (Kadesjo and Gillberg 2001) have shown that in the ADHD/DCD group 58 per cent had a poor outcome compared with 13 per cent in their comparison group ($p < 0.001$). Remaining symptoms of ADHD, antisocial personality disorder, alcohol abuse, criminal offending, reading disorders and low educational level were over-represented in the ADHD/DCD groups and the co-existence of both conditions together has a gloomier prognosis.

- Take up a non-competitive sport as a family. A sport where you have to work as a team can work well where there is not one member being particularly highlighted.

- Rambling or orienteering can be done as a family group.

- Learn salsa or line dancing together.

- Dance mats linked to a 'play station' can be fun and can help with dance skills and even with sequencing.

- Different non-team sports may be a route to success. These may include sports such as badminton, canoeing, archery, skiing, golf and swimming. The individual does not need to be judged against their peers and can learn to self-measure their progress.

- If the adolescent is reluctant to participate in sport with others it may be worth considering trying a gym – a personal trainer can provide one-to-one support and a tailored programme of exercises to improve stamina and co-ordination. Use of walking/running machines, and static cycles do not require excellent co-ordination and can even be used while watching television or listening to music.

Negative narratives

How do things that have happened to us during our life, shape the way we feel about ourselves? When does what other people say about us become more important than how we feel about our self and who we see we are. For some of us, we grow up with a certainty and a belief that we are 'OK', and that others are not always right. Enough good things happen on a day-to-day basis to tell us this, and others confirm this as well. However, if the external comments are coming fast and sharp, it is harder to have time to re-balance the negative perceptions. If this happens too often, we begin to believe others rather than ourselves.

'Life sentences'

Adults who have grown up with the knowledge that they were 'different' in a time when DCD didn't seem to exist, tell of the importance of gaining acknowledgement and recognition for the struggle they had been through. The chance to take on a new persona and recognise that they have strengths as well as difficulties can for some individuals turn on a light bulb. It may allow them to see themselves for the first time as a person with a difficulty and not a difficult person as may have been portrayed by others.

During their school days many adults will have been physically or verbally bullied. This may result in the individual having a view that frames the way he approaches tasks or his learning. Each one of us at some time will have received a negative comment about ourselves in front of peers as either a child or adult. When I trained as a doctor, I remember receiving regular ritual humiliation in front of fellow students as well as patients. This was seen as a routine method of teaching. I can still feel the blushes and remember what was said and by whom. These events can leave a lasting impression throughout your life: from then onwards you may never believe you are able to learn this particular subject or topic area. This fixed perception may stay with you, lasting even until your own children are learning a similar subject some 30 years later and asking you for your help. You may even hear yourself saying 'but I can't do that' or 'I have never been very good at that'.

Random phrases can form scars and act as 'life sentences'. Most of us have one or two experiences of these life sentences. However, we learn to balance this with other positive responses from others, and end up with a total view. In contrast, the child with DCD and other specific learning difficulties may have received numerous comments since early child-hood. They are usually not forgotten after a few hours but remain with the person and shape the way he feels about himself, and how others may see him as well.

'You're useless at football, we don't want you in the team.'

'Spaz – you can't even catch the ball.'

'You must be pretty thick if you write like that!'

'How many times do I need to tell you – can't you even listen to simple instructions?'

'Write it out again and try harder next time, your writing is so difficult to read.'

'I am afraid you can't come to camp as you will be too slow to keep up with the others.'

'Don't ask Jo to put the pictures up, they are sure to fall down.'

'You can't do that, give it to your sister, she is much better at that sort of thing.'

Fixed perceptions

Before moving on with life, the individual with DCD may need to re-write his life sentences in order for him to gain a more positive and balanced picture. If this is not done, he may go forward seeing only the negative aspects of his character and being unable to see or believe he has strengths as well.

The consequences of this are sometimes seen in adults who chose jobs and courses that on reflection may seem rather to be the one to avoid. For example, an adult with DCD chose to be an accountant when he had actually failed mathematics in school. Another person chose a job as a receptionist, thinking that this would be right for her with her excellent communication skills. But the work also meant organising and recording information, when her sequencing and organisational skills were poor. This is why it can be difficult at times to make career choices. Individuals may have some skills which may be ideal for the job, while at the same time have other difficulties that present enormous barriers to success.

- In working with the adolescent, it is important to ascertain what life sentences he believes are real and remain fixed.

- How true are they in all conditions and all times?

- Could the individual see his strengths as well, to be able to start to change the balance?

- Are they fixed beliefs and how could they be altered?

6 Raising Self-esteem and Improving Social Skills

A man cannot be comfortable without his own approval.

Mark Twain

Introduction

Self-esteem is talked about a great deal, and strategies for improving it are often mooted. However, in considering self-esteem it is important to consider both 'self-concept' and 'self-esteem', both referring to conception of self, but self-concept is the informational part of the conception (what we know or believe about ourselves) and self-esteem is the emotional part (how we feel about ourselves). In addition, self-talk also deals with the internal dialogue that everyone carries on with themselves ('talking to ourselves').

The adolescent with DCD may have a running internal dialogue that sees himself as having less worth, and may have poor self-concept because of years of seeing himself as simply different from his peers and unable to join in with social and physical activities with ease.

It is essential that the individual becomes self-motivated and has a reason to change his present state and work on ways to improve skills and attitudes. This has to start with what is important to him first at this time, rather than what may seem important to others. If this is addressed, he will begin to take control over his actions rather than waiting for the answers from someone else.

Cognitive models have been used in adolescents with ADHD and DCD and have been seen to be a practical way of enhancing daily functioning and raising self-esteem (Stevenson *et al.* 2002; Willoughby *et al.* 2000).

Seeking successful outcomes from negative experiences

The adolescent may be aware that he is not being asked to parties or out shopping with peers and so may feel hurt and rejected. Less practice and less opportunity for being sociable leads to a self-fulfilling prophecy of being less socially able and so on...

There is a need for successful social outcomes for the adolescent with DCD, so that he can see and feel success and build on this. This may need an adult to work with him to help to plan and achieve this and suggest ideas of where he may go, and even accompany him the first time to get him across the threshold. A more structured setting such as going to the cinema or going bowling may be a better way to gain success at this stage, as the individual does not have to plan and consider what to do as well as trying to interact with his peers. It is better to try social situations one-to-one before trying a group situation such as having a party. This allows as a parent greater ability to oversee, even from a distance and recover situations if they are getting out of control.

Discussing feelings and acknowledging them and discussing ways that they could change is important if the individual is to have positive modelling experiences – this can be done through role playing and asking a series of key questions to open the discussion.

- What went well this afternoon?
- What do you think didn't go as well as you expected?
- How could you do it differently next time?

When talking to the individual it is important to discuss what is possible for him and what feels right to him, instead of what others think he should do. 'Shoulds' distract us from identifying and fulfilling our own needs, abilities, interests and personal goals. Find out what he wants to do and what he could be good at, value his decisions, and take actions, even if they have to be small steps first, designed to fulfil this potential.

Rewards and goals should be set by the individual rather than by others – but they must be realistic and achievable. This may need to be discussed, and tasks broken down into reasonable chunks. Create a whole-picture vision so that the individual knows what he is aiming for, and then help him to put the smaller steps in place. The adolescent might benefit from an opportunity to have a mentor that he feels can act as an advocate. Peer–peer mentorship can work well, if carefully selected. It can be someone a year or two older who understands the need for support, and is acknowledged for the help given. Or it could be someone outside the immediate family (e.g. a grandparent).

- **Test for reality**. Try to get the individual to separate the emotional reactions based on past experience – these may show as fears, anxieties and bad feelings – from the reality of the current situation. Encourage him to ask others close to him for a reality check.

- **Encourage** the individual to take safe chances but to expect some failures – this is normal for all of us and should be seen in that context.

- **List the successes** and remind the individual of what he can do, not just what he can't.

- **Encourage the adolescent to start to list five good things** about himself, however small, and add to the list. When the individual is being self-critical, encourage him to look at the problem and not see himself as the problem.

- **Reinforce** positive self-talk – celebrate success however small.

- **Give the adolescent the skills to wipe away negative self-talk.**

- Encourage **responsibility and decision making** – even if mistakes are made, explain that we all learn from mistakes, e.g. we fall several times before we walk properly, we learn to drive a car gradually and only improve with practice.

- See when **small positive steps** have been made and encourage the individual to think what that feels like.

- **Talk but also listen** to the individual about him believing that he is important and a valued member of the class or family.

- **Encourage the individual to be nice to himself, rewarding** himself when something has gone well.

- Work with the individual to **build a vision** of his future.

- **Discuss what he likes in others and how he would like others to see him.**

- **Look at the posture of the individual.** Does he look confident? How could he improve this to appear confident to others?

- **Forget past failures** – don't be trapped in the past. Each individual can start again and should be given the chance.

Supporting the development of social skills

The aim of nearly every parent is to move their child over the hurdles of adolescence to adulthood and on to independent living. Skills need to be acquired in a number of areas in order to get there, and may mean that it takes longer to get to the end goal.

It is important to understand what are the keys to meeting and social-ising with others in teen years. If social skills are not addressed there is a risk that the individual will chose *any* friends that show interest in him or her (not always appropriately) rather than the ones that really fit into his or her lifestyle and way of life. Social skills are best gained in a 'normal' environment where interaction feels relaxed and not forced. However it is sometimes useful to practise techniques in smaller groups to learn the social rules before launching out into the big wide world.

In considering where the individual may have difficulties with social communication, the five areas that need to be explored to ensure success-ful communication are the following:

- conversational skills
- making and maintaining friendships
- understanding the 'hidden curriculum'
- assertive conversation
- repairing conversation.

Conversational skills

These skills include initiating a conversation, continuing and ending conversations, the ability to switch subjects and maintain interest, reservicocity of conversation (listening as well as answering).

- Using a video or audio tape can allow the individual to gain insight into the strengths and weaknesses of his or her social interaction.

- Other video materials are useful as a means of discussing different social scenarios.

- There are social skills programmes on CD-ROM such as 'Mindreading' that can be used to practise these skills, but need to be contextualised to the experiences of the individual so that skills gained can be transferred into a real situation.

Making and maintaining friendships

Understanding about social distance and picking up non-verbal cues are key to this.

- Feedback on social faux pas is important, undertaken in a safe non-threatening atmosphere, so that the individual can improve in a similar setting in the future.

- Social rehearsal can also be used to practise openers and closers in the conversation.

Understanding the 'hidden curriculum'

Social do's and don'ts are not always written as rules.

- This is difficult for the individual who lacks non-verbal skills and does not recognise idiom, sarcasm and metaphor. These may need to be taught formally so that different scenarios are practised to allow a framework to develop.

- Writing down some key rules for home and school helps to see what behaviour is acceptable in differing environments, but also allows for discussions for when this may change (e.g. running in the corridor in school is not allowed, apart from when there is a fire).

Assertive conversation

Being able to get ideas, thoughts and views across in a non-threatening manner and being aware of not over-dominating a conversation.

- This is a skill that can be practised. Using audio and video tape allows the individual to see when their tone may tell a different story from the one they want to portray and allows him or her to alter tone, pace and volume and become more aware.

Repairing conversations

This is an essential skill to learn. Some teenagers will go into a situation too fast and not stop and think about the implications of their actions and words until it is too late. Learning to repair and rewind are skills that need gentle support as they can feel very painful to the individual when they are aware of the damage they may have made to an already delicate relationship.

- Gaining awareness of social mistakes is the first step in preventing future ones.

- Talking about the situation and what went wrong and creating a strategy for the future can allow the individual to gain confidence.

- Asking for advice from a number of safe sources on what to say and how to say it allows a consensus on managing a situation. It may be worth discussing who is 'safe' to ask, who will be honest but discreet.

- Rehearsal if the individual is unsure is always a good idea.

- Acknowledging that we can all make mistakes allows the individual to know that he is not the only one. He should not feel too upset about the situation and should use it as a positive learning tool.

A tool to help map social hierarchies

In order to understand how an individual relates to different people, there is a need to 'see' a social order. We talk to different people in different ways. You use language with your peers that you usually know is inappropriate with your parents! However, if this is not clearly understood, serious social gaffes can arise with major consequences. The head teacher in a school can be insulted if a child says 'Hi' in an over-familiar way and may misunderstand the reason for this.

Social touches are also different. For example you may kiss and hug a parent but should not do this to a stranger.

The individual needs to have a visual model of how to behave with different people and at different times, so that he can understand the rules and then learn to behave in the most appropriate way. This will be different in different cultures, and the individual needs to understand the 'norm' where he is and then learn variations from this once this is achieved.

Using a 'Social Bull's Eye'

1. Create a list with the individual of people who mean something to him (parents, siblings, close friends, trainer/teacher, and relatives) and why he thinks that is so, e.g. what makes them different from each other.

2. Map this onto which groups these individuals belong to.

3. Consider why they are important and why the individual needs a balance of different friends and relationships.

4. Talk about how he behaves with different groups and who else he may meet and how he would behave with a stranger compared to a friend.

The individual may be helped mapping his own relationships to see where he has friends but also where he fits in with others in his life. Once this has been mapped, it is useful to discuss how he sees the different relationships and how they interact with each other. Does he see this in a positive or negative light? Where does he see difficulties arise? This gives an opportunity to gain an insight into the adolescent's frame of thinking and is an opportunity to discuss ways of reframing if needed.

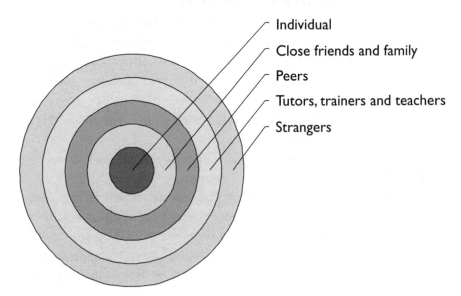

Figure 6.1 The Social Bull's Eye

An alternative to the bull's eye approach is to use chairs and physically move them into different positions in the room and discuss distance, and language differences in different relationships. This could be played like a 'mock party' and can be used in a social skills group even with young adolescents.

Meeting people and trying new hobbies and interests

The individual may find it harder to be successful in any one area in school and may find that he wants to look for interests away from the academic environment. The pleasure and success gained from a well-chosen hobby can spill over into the classroom. It can also be used as a potential topic of conversation and allow others to perceive the young person in a different way.

The following are suggestions for hobbies that adolescents with DCD are more likely to see success with. Any hobby can be tried but may need to be learned at a slower pace and component parts of the skills required learned separately before all being put together. An empathic and encouraging trainer is the route to success.

Badminton	Canoeing	Horse-riding	Rambling
Dog walking	Cookery	Photography	Yoga/Pilates
Drama	Fencing	Golf	T'ai Chi
Martial arts	Drums	Swimming	Computing

If the individual does not make progress quickly, think about returning to the activity later on when his skills have improved. Slow progress is better than no progress. Let the individual measure himself against himself rather than against others.

Case study

Mark was 16 years of age and his 14-year-old sister went out every week to a disco on a Sunday evening and left Mark at home playing on his computer. At school he had one friend who he talked to at lunchtime, but had little in common with the other boys in his class who liked playing football. He lacked the conversation to join in, or sometimes just seemed to try too hard and get it wrong. A joke he may have told at home would go completely flat if told to others in school.

Mark would have liked to play football when they knocked about at lunchtime, but he was laughed at when he had tried a few years before and decided it was better to wander around alone. He had gained weight over the past couple of years and now did not feel very attractive at all. He wanted to go out, even to see a film, but really did not have anyone to go with.

He was introduced by his father, who was a keen golfer, to the local golf range on a Sunday morning. Over a year Mark very gradually learned how to use the clubs and began to play an occasional game with his father. It did not matter that he was still learning, as the handicap system allowed him to play alongside his dad. He also got to know people down at the club and eventually had a Saturday job collecting the balls on the range and tidying up.

Mark was still very much a loner at school. He found it was difficult having conversations with the others in his class. At 16 years of age after his GCSEs, Mark went to college and over the summer he worked at the golf range and became fitter. This helped him to gain confidence when going to college and ask for help from his tutors there, and explain to them that he needed help with recording work because his writing was still very poor. For Mark's parents this was the first sign that Mark was growing up. However, he still needed to be accepted by his peer group and needed to learn the social rules, when to talk and when to listen. This did not come easy for him.

7 Transition

Change is not made without inconvenience, even from worse to better.

Richard Hooker

Don't fear change, embrace it.

Anthony J. D'Angelo

If you never change your mind, why have one?

Edward DeBono

Adolescence is a period of rapid changes.
Between the ages of 12 and 17, for example, a parent ages as
much as 20 years.

Anon

Introduction

Teenage years are a time of trial and tribulation, as the teenager is learning to adapt to changes both emotionally and physically. For the individual with specific learning difficulties, the time is made worse by trying to cope with many of the problems that he may have encountered in primary school, but are now accentuated as he moves into the secondary school system. He may be less emotionally mature than his peers and therefore be more exposed on arrival at secondary school and less protected than in previous years.

Most adolescents want to be like their peers. The adolescent with DCD may not yet be at a stage where he can see that this is important and this makes him stand apart from his class. He may not be able to work in a social situation with confidence and if given the choice may be happiest and feel safest when at home. This is in contrast to most teenagers' behaviour. They may even want to actively increase their distance from their parents and join up with their peers and some would even try to disown their parents altogether if they could! This is a normal part of adolescence development and a part of gaining your own identity, with its likes and dislikes. However for the adolescent already with lowered self-esteem and confidence at this vulnerable stage, the difference between the individual boy with DCD and his peers seems to widen for some years.

Within the classroom, if we compare the different learning styles of three 14 year olds in a class – this difference can seem even more pronounced. A 14 year old girl may be a mature independent learner, compare this with the average 14 year old boy who may need some guidance with his learning. Further contrast this to the 14 year old boy with DCD who may need to be given information in small pieces, suitably chunked and require guidance at all stages of his learning.

These differences lessen as the individual emerges from the teenage years but can make this time painful for the individual and his family as the contrast becomes more pronounced.

Gentle support to increase independence is important but balanced with the need for continued background support – a fine balance.

Transition points

Most transitions are difficult for the adolescent. If he finds it harder to make smooth transitions from task to task, then moving from one situation to another such as moving from primary school to secondary school will represent a huge leap in the dark. Preparation for the child and those who are supporting him will help increase the chances of success.

For most children, adapting to the changes of a new school environment may take a week or two, but for others such as the adolescent with DCD, it may well take months to settle down and grasp the variety of different situations that are taking place. It may also cause increasing signs of anxiety before the move, as past experiences will reinforce knowledge of future difficulties.

Transition points in the adolescent's life cause different sets of difficulties at each stage and need to be carefully planned for.

Key transition points

- from primary to secondary school
- from secondary school to further/higher education
- leaving home and gaining independent living skills
- gaining employment and staying in employment
- forming relationships.

Planning for transition

The key to success, is to start early and ensure there is a team approach including both the parents and the child in this process. The move for any child means major adaptations.

If there has been little preparation for these huge changes that occur between primary and secondary school then the child may start to flounder. For some, the supportive environment of primary school may have meant there were few difficulties until this time.

If difficulties arise, this can result in the child not accessing the curriculum adequately, and this can also impact in the playground making it harder for him to make friends at a crucial time in developing the new peer group. Late or little preparation, may result in lasting damage throughout the secondary school days.

For the child with recognised needs there may have been a plan put together. For the child not identified, there will obviously be no plan to support the child.

The length of time the child requires support at this stage may be difficult for some to understand. There may be a reticence to continue and a feeling that the child should be able to go it alone after a few weeks in school. For some adolescents there may be a need for low-level but continued support throughout school days. A graded plan of action with regular review points and new goals being set as progress is made ensures that the individual continues to receive support for as long as he requires it. It is important to ensure the student is at the centre of the decision-making process in how support is given and what he feels are his difficulties. Often it is the organisational skills that impact most at this time.

Making a plan

In order to plan a successful transition for the individual from primary school to secondary school and from school to college or workplace, adequate and comprehensive planning needs to take place. The individuals involved will vary at different ages and stages, but essentially it should be an interdisciplinary process involving the adolescent at the centre of the decision-making process.

Key elements of the plan

When should the plan start?

Who needs to be involved?

How should it be acted on?

How should it be communicated to others?

What are you aiming to achieve?

Who needs to see the plan?

Ideally, the following people need to be involved in the process of transition planning:

- the young person

- parents

- school/college staff

- careers service

- education services.

In addition, other individuals can be brought in if they have had prior involvement: social workers (if applicable or other associated services), health service personnel, educational psychologists, personnel from supported employment schemes or training programmes, and voluntary agency staff.

Start with the strengths and realities of the situation:

- internal motivation and past experiences that may colour the individual's career planning process

- hobbies and interests – successful experiences to build upon

- area living in or could live in – e.g. are there relatives in a larger city with greater choice of training/employment if the individual is living currently in a rural setting?

- levels of independent living skills the individual has – could they live away from home, or do they need to still remain within a family setting?

- course availability – there may be limitations in the area on the range of courses

- particular colleges with greater experience of special needs or with specific learning resources that could be of help

- parental expectation – is this realistic?

In addition you should ask:

- Is the individual realistic about his or her strengths?

- Can he see where he would like to be in the next few years?

- Are you realistic about what he has difficulties with and what support will be required in order for him to meet his objectives?

- Who needs to give support and how often and how is this best delivered?

Where may problems arise?

- Individuals may not have the ability to assert their own views and ideas.

- They may have unrealistic career aspirations.

- They may not see they have strengths and go for an inappropriate course.

- The presence of a team approach to support may be overwhelming for the individual.

- Presenting real options and choices and constructing the steps required to reach success takes time and may need some negotiation.

- Low-level but essential help such as organisational support may be overlooked.

What are other barriers that may impact on the plan?

- Personal life – problems at home may have an impact on what can be achieved.

- Work – the individual may have very specific views regarding the area he or she wants to work in, e.g. wants to work with animals.

- Living arrangements – these may be fixed because of social, economic or health reasons, e.g. needs to be near home because requires parental support.

- Fears – for example difficulty in using transport or handling money, may limit the possibility of going for some courses further afield. These skills may need to be checked and taught to ensure that this is not *the* barrier for success.

Positive routes to success

Take a lead from the individual to see what is important to him rather than what others say is important.

Appropriate careers guidance is essential, tailored to strengths and motivation – the end goal may have to be broken down into smaller steps to ensure a successful outcome and allow the individual to gain the necessary suite of skills.

Pre-training skills may need to be acquired before launching on further education, such as study skills, money management, using public transport, use of adaptive technology to ensure that the individual can take notes.

Work experience – appropriate work placement may be difficult to find, it requires greater planning and support. If the individual has to make his own approaches it may seem daunting. Help and support may need to be given, and the individual taken and stayed with to ensure that his needs are met and instructions given in a way that he can understand and carry out.

It is important to provide monitoring and feedback after work placement. A work placement can provide the first stage for assessing the appropriateness of a type of work for the individual with DCD. Positive and negative experiences need to be fed back to those training the individual to ensure a future work placement is nearer to the type of work the individual will eventually want to work in.

Coping with changing situations

Change is the one thing that is constant in our lives and the one thing that makes the individual with DCD wobble. Not knowing what to expect next can feel very nerve-racking. It is important to understand the consequent behaviour when the individual is constantly on guard in case something else changes in his life.

Executive functioning

Executive functions are those abilities needed for problem solving. As one moves into adolescence these skills are essential for success. If they are not present, it can lead others to see the individual as lazy or oppositional.

Becoming a competent adult means that it is necessary to cope with new situations presented to you as well as being able to learn from past mistakes. The ability to be both flexible and adaptable in differing social situations allows you to cope in new circumstances with confidence.

The individual with DCD may display great difficulty in coping with change, unable quickly to see the differences in the surroundings and react with speed. He may also find that he repeats behaviour that was not productive last time, even though at a cognitive level he knows it is wrong to do so. It is as if he has no brakes at times and just launches in, feeling remorseful afterwards that he has made the same mistakes again and again.

He may be feeling agitated and overwhelmed and, rather than asking for help, will refuse to do a task and this may result in him behaving in a way that is 'uncool'.

The adolescent may also be seen to have something called *executive dysfunctioning*. This may affect half the adolescents with DCD. The following are the key features:

- **poor cognitive flexibility** – difficulty leaping from one idea to another

- **lack of adjustment of behaviour using environmental feedback** – being able to learn from experiences around you

- **difficulty extracting social rules from experiences** – seeing the implied rule rather than the explicit one (the individual may have been in a similar situation before but does not seem to learn from it and ends up making the same mistakes)

- **difficulty in selecting essential from non-essential information** – the individual sees all the information at the same level of importance and finds it hard to 'sieve' it according to priority or see what may be risky

- **impaired working memory** – this may make it harder to hold on to several pieces of information at one time and juggle information – the individual also can't juggle several different tasks at once

- **difficulty in organisation and completing tasks** may prevent the individual even trying to begin the task.

Assessing how much support is enough support

Assessing the level and type of support can be difficult, so also is understanding where that should take place and with whom. However, the setting up of an appropriate environment is important for individual success. Every child will need different levels of support. There is no *classic DCD adolescent.* He may in addition have other difficulties such as ADHD, and language-processing difficulties that may also additionally impact on his learning.

The support given to a visually impaired or a physically disabled child would ensure that the environment for the child was appropriate, and there would not be an expectation that the child would have to fit the environment. In this context, we would not consider taking a white stick away on the assumption it was no longer needed, or even break it in two to share it with two children! There is a clear understanding that the individual would require long-term support and would not necessarily have mastered his way around school and may continue to require support throughout his school days.

DCD in some senses can be considered in similar ways to other learning disabilities – it does not just go away suddenly one day. However the DCD child is not instantly obvious to others and does not walk around with a marker of his difficulties, so is often seen in a different light and may even in the past have been seen as lazy, stupid or not really trying as hard as he could.

'How many times should he be shown?'

'He should be able to understand it by now.'

'I am not going to mother him any longer.'

'He needs to learn to do it for himself one day.'

Low-level but continuing intervention can make the difference between success and failure, especially where there are constant choices and changes occurring. Many individuals with DCD can learn a skill in one environment but find it hard to adapt this learning to a new environment. Change is the greatest constant threat to the stability of the adolescent. Consistency means providing a level playing field for development.

Coping with the process of change

Secondary schools are often places of change. Desks and chairs are moved in the class, relief teachers come in to cover lessons. Rules vary from one lesson to another, some implicit and some explicit.

For example, the implied rule may be difficult for the adolescent to take on board as he may not pick up the social cues and nuances of the language needed to do so – knowing what language to use with different people such as the head teacher versus a peer, or understanding the differences between different teachers' teaching styles. These can cause additional strains on the child who is also trying to cope with a number of underlying difficulties and now has extra problems layered on top. This can mean the adolescent has little reserve capacity, resulting in a breakdown in the child's mechanisms for coping and possibly why we sometimes see secondary school as being a crisis time, after the child has seemingly been able to cope in primary school.

Understanding the rules

Understanding the rules is essential in any setting. The school rules may be written down and told to the pupils when they start. The 'alternative rules' are the unspoken set that every school has. It is the code of behaviour – standing in one class, sitting in another, greeting a teacher informally, or saying 'Sir' after every sentence. The child with difficulties in interpreting social distance and social hierarchy may also have problems interpreting metaphor. Common phrases in the classroom can cause confusion and misinterpretation for the adolescent with DCD and result in the individual not knowing how to respond. A response may appear rude to some, as it may be abrupt and then the child may make further mistakes by attempting to patch up the problem he has caused.

> 'Just pull yourself together.'
>
> 'You are lippy.'
>
> 'Don't bite off more than you can chew.'
>
> 'You're barking up the wrong tree.'
>
> 'You put your foot in your mouth then.'
>
> 'Your ears must be burning.'

The Big Move

The child moving to secondary school may be:

- already identified as having DCD and now needing a smooth transition plan from primary to secondary school to receive continuing support

- not yet identified and starting to fail once arriving in secondary school

- recognised and referred to health professionals, only to find out there is a long waiting list or no service for his age group but still needing his functional and educational difficulties to be addressed

- recognised in school as being difficult rather than having difficulties, and seen as 'a behaviour problem'

- recognised in school and given support, understanding and help with motor co-ordination and related difficulties

- seen as average, as he has dropped down into that range, and so not seen as a priority, when in fact he has potentially superior abilities if these were appropriately supported.

The move to secondary school may expose the child to difficulties at key times in the day such as coping alone in the playground at break and lunchtimes. Teachers may not be present all of the time to supervise in the same way as in the primary school playground. In addition, not all teachers in a large school will be aware of the child's difficulties. Lacking the necessary skills in sports activities may make him a target for bullying from other adolescents in school. If he has been bullied either physically or verbally this may add to a layer of existing anxiety.

The feelings of anxiety about lack of control of his environment can lead to panic and may have a knock-on effect on the individual's behaviour in a number of ways that may at times be misinterpreted by others. For example, he may lash out without obvious reason or withdraw into himself in a form of self-protection. He may be then perceived by others as having behavioural problems. Alternatively he may become chronically anxious and may develop symptoms and signs of depression.

- If change is predicted, e.g. school trips, changes of teachers, discuss these with the child so that he knows what may happen (as far as possible) – record this for him as well as telling him verbally and show pictures if necessary to reinforce the individual's understanding.

- If change is unplanned – still try to inform the child what may happen to give some framework for him to cope with.

In order to ensure that appropriate support is given, it is essential that parents and teachers have an understanding of how difficulties may present and what areas are going to be hardest for the adolescent. An understanding of this can have a huge impact on the way the individual is supported and can cause a paradigm shift in the attitudes of others. The adolescent may be presenting one picture to the outside world but may not be portraying truly how hard he is really trying and how difficult it is for him on a day-to-day basis.

Key areas entering secondary school

- Navigation around a new school with several buildings
- Meeting new children who may not understand or be aware of his difficulties
- Meeting new teachers who do not recognise that he has difficulties
- Learning about the rules of the school – both explicit and implicit
- Learning new teachers' names and understanding their expectations and their different styles of teaching
- Carrying equipment around all day with him – no central place to return to – therefore increasing the chances of losing equipment or not having correct equipment for the next class
- Locker far away from lessons
- Coping with change determined by others not him
- The need to organise work and manage his way from class to class
- The shift to team games and away from ball skills
- Less supervision in the playground and at lunchtime
- Canteen or packed lunches with less supervision
- New subjects to be studied
- Faster pace of delivery of information, need for faster recording speeds and comprehension
- Coping with greater time pressures – such as essay writing, examinations

Checklists for transition

In preparing an identified child with DCD for the move to secondary school, a transition plan is essential to ensure all areas of need are covered. The checklists below provide schools and parents with a list of potential areas to be planned for.

Outline of school and details of the school day

- Information should be transferred from primary school so that all new teachers have a profile of strengths and difficulties and what has been of help to the child in primary school. This could be kept in a 'share care' diary and could then be added to as additional information is gathered from one class teacher to another, indicating what techniques help the child.

- Arrangement for visits to school should ideally take place over two terms to allow the child to build a picture of the school and its layout.

- A map of the school could be provided; in addition, photos of key areas could be taken to allow the child to become more familiar with the school setting.

- It is useful to allow parents to be given the opportunity to visit the school.

- The school timetable with teachers' names (and photos if possible) should be given as soon as possible.

- Location of lockers needs to be considered. The child may be slower navigating his way around school and may be more disorganised. Long distances may mean he ends up being late for lessons or may lose belongings as he compensates by carrying everything around with him all the time (spare locker keys are usually essential).

Assessment of needs and development of an Individual Learning Plan (ILP)

- A risk assessment should be undertaken and adaptations planned for before arrival.

- A baseline assessment should ideally be undertaken to check where the child's learning level is, and an ILP created to include the level of remedial support required including a consideration for differentiation in P.E. and other sports.

- Study skills training may need to be planned in order for the child to be able to plan and lay out work appropriately, e.g. in the areas of essay writing, homework recording and note taking.

- Adaptations need to be considered in all subjects especially where new skills may need to be acquired such as chemistry. (The child may need to stand rather than sit or may need to work in a pair for practical tasks.)

- IT requirements also need to be ascertained and the appropriate training given so that the child can easily use new programs or equipment when in a classroom. This needs to be started with sufficient time to allow the child to gain confidence and ability in using the equipment and the software, e.g. voice-activated software, organiser software.

After assessment and starting off at school

- Use of specially adapted tools, such as a ridged ruler that can be easily held, a circular protractor that can grip the paper, and pens with a rubber gripper to help with writing, can help the individual access the curriculum more easily.

- Lunchtime and break-time arrangements. This may mean offering the individual a 'safe place' to retire to at times of increased anxiety.

- Plans for an adapted P.E. curriculum may need to be made as the individual may not be able to participate in team games.

- Practical consideration also needs to be given such as where the individual will recharge his laptop between classes or print materials that he has recorded.

- If a mentor/tutor or peer-to-peer relationship is being introduced, then ideally an introduction should be made before the start of the new term.

- Reduced volume allowance for homework.

- Homework recorded and books put into bag.

- Position and seating for the child should be considered. This may include use of angle boards, position in class, amount of room required, where the individual is placed, type of seating, seating wedge.

Preparation for examinations

- Extra time allowance in examinations may need to be considered.

- The need for an amanuensis for external examinations and tests in school needs to be considered. If agreed, then the child needs time to practise the skills required.

Home/school liaison

- A clear communications strategy between home and school should be set up and agreed between all parties to allow for an active parent partnership.

- Consider uniform changes – ties to be worn, different fastenings, lace-up shoes – that may lead to delay getting to class or games lessons.

- Suitable packed lunch that can be easily opened and eaten.

Case study

John was 14 years of age and had already been 'expelled' from three schools. His mother was at her wit's end not knowing what to do next. He had said he wanted to go to one particular school. After copious arrangements and planning, and as he was very talented using computers, he even gained a scholarship there.

He had most recently been expelled after one term at the boarding school for a run of misdemeanours, culminating in being caught smoking marijuana with some other boys on school property. He did not cope with change well and showed increasing signs of anxiety, but at the same time angry outbursts, usually directed at his parents.

The educational psychologist assessed John and had shown that he had a very high oral IQ but when it came to getting it down on paper it was a disaster. His writing was impossible to read and he struggled to complete any assignments. At times in class, John would call out the answers even before the teacher had prompted the class. His impulsiveness and risk-taking behaviour was now reaching a point that was impacting on his ability to gain any examinations. Without formal qualifications John would find it hard to reach his goal of running his own IT company. He had already told his parents he would need a personal assistant to organise him.

On his 15th birthday, John was again excluded from school. During the summer his parents moved back to the area in the North of England where they used to live. The local education authority was running an innovative and individualised programme for individuals that had been excluded from school and John was allowed to join it. He was treated as an adult but he had to attend daily. He had to do basic GSCEs but was allowed to attend a college for advanced computer programming. A laptop was supplied to him and support to help him organise his time. Six months later John was still attending and heading towards his first set of qualifications.

8 Strategies for Secondary School

Introduction

Personal care

What areas may affect the adolescent with DCD?
    Are the foundation skills in place?
    Auditory memory – A problem?
    Difficulties with mathematics

The school environment
    Larger school
    Larger class size
    No desks or lockers

Different subjects, different approaches, different people

Independent travel

Homework

Time concepts

Organisational skills

Lunch

Preparing for statutory examinations
  Strategies for revising for examinations
  Checklists
  Advice on special arrangements for external examinations
  Other techniques for studying

Making career choices and planning for further education

Success is a journey, not a destination.

Ben Sweetland

Introduction

Teenagers with DCD, while being intellectually equal to their peers, are often emotionally younger by several years. They still require reassurance and support more in keeping with a child 2–3 years younger than their chronological age. This gap widens from the age of 13 years until late teenage years, which can be the hardest time in the life of the individual with DCD. He or she is trying to cope with all the changes that are occurring but lacks the maturity to take these changes on board. The option to mix with younger children in primary school is removed when he or she goes to secondary school. He may feel that he really can't fully mix with his peers until he reaches his twenties.

Moving from a small local primary school where a child is well known by staff, to a large secondary school can be scary for most children. However, for the child with DCD, every change has an impact on his ability to settle down, to be assimilated into the school and to learn effectively. The combined effect of many changes occurring all at once can have a lasting detrimental effect if this is not carefully planned and the child not supported.

Successful secondary schooling is dependent on support from the point the individual arrives at school. Highlighting who may need this support and at what level, requires a process of screening so that a detailed Individual Education Plan can be drawn up and the steps to success outlined. The teenager must be integral to the process so that it is geared to where he thinks he requires the most support. Many of the hotspots in school are not only problems for the child with DCD but also for many other individuals arriving at a large establishment and getting to know their way around.

Personal care

The impact of poor personal care can spill over into school or the work-place and affect relationships and others' perceptions of the individual. Many individuals going through teenage years lack interest in seemingly boring tasks of cleanliness; others will be over-zealous and take hours in the bathroom. (Some individuals may have associated symptoms of obsessive compulsive disorder.) Compromise and appropriateness has to be the name of the game.

Organising himself and the bedroom may seem a mammoth task for the individual. In the rush of the morning trying to find what he needs for his school day e.g. clothes that match, socks the right colour may make the adolescent regularly late for school and create high tension in the house-hold.

- Labelling of drawers, and use of Polaroid photos to make finding items easier can be used.

- Plan in advance what is to be worn – don't leave it to the last moment.

- Master and practise new fasteners/buttons while clothes are removed.

- Match clothes with the event and abilities.

- Practise tasks without vision – doing up zips and the top buttons on a shirt.

- Use easy-care fabrics and clothes without fastenings.

- Use alternatives to traditional fastenings – poppers and Velcro are easier to undo.

- Make sure the individual is balanced first when getting dressed. Consider sitting on the floor when dressing.

- Check which is the back and front of the garment – look for the label or a logo to act as a reminder.

- Shave – built-in safety guards and electric shavers are useful.

- Establish a routine so that tasks become automatic.

- Prepare in advance – avoid a rush, better to get up five minutes earlier and get to the destination on time, than rush and feel sweaty and panic-stricken.

- Plan drawers – put things in the order that they will be put on, have a clothes horse to hang them on.

- Make separators in the drawers so everything doesn't just fall on top of one another, or use baskets to separate items out.

- Seat for the shower – consider sitting down to shower.

- Place a mat in the shower to stop slipping.

What areas may affect the adolescent with DCD?

The adolescent with DCD can be affected in many or all areas of schooling. This may stem from internal difficulties such as lacking the foundation skills necessary to cope with the faster pace or to changes that are happening around him that he is not adequately prepared for.

Navigating around a larger school, getting to know teachers and their teaching styles and greater expectations on the volume and quality of work can put the individual under continued pressure.

Particular areas of difficulty may be in subjects such as mathematics where the language and understanding of shape concepts may be harder as well as the practical implications of using a ruler or protractor.

The individual may also have difficulties with the volume of information being offered to him and have difficulty in processing this only through listening, i.e. through the auditory route, and may need to be shown what to do or have a visual reminder.

Are the foundation skills in place?

Secondary school usually means a faster pace. There are examinations to prepare for and results to attain. This means that in class there is no longer handwriting practice but the need to take notes down at speed with accuracy and legibility. If writing skills are poor, this will have an impact on the individual when he comes to review his work, when he may be unable to read his own writing.

This means his notes may have little value when it comes to revision and examinations. He then has to work harder gaining that information when revising and may end up having to rely solely on textbooks.

Auditory memory – A problem?

The youngster may also have auditory memory and processing difficulties, which mean that he may miss out on information given to him in class, seemingly hearing the first bit and the last piece of a story but missing the middle part. This ends up with the child not being able to access the lesson fully and again having to catch up at home, working twice as hard to keep up with his peers.

Difficulties with mathematics

The child may have weaker mathematical skills and not have the foundation skills in place to move on to more complex mathematics. Weaker mathematics skills are more common in children with DCD and may be linked to a difficulty in visualising abstract concepts. Building up concepts of shape and form may be difficult to do, for example in geometry where the student has to think about geometric shapes and what they would look like if they were rotated around a central point. For the individual with DCD, first seeing the shape and then secondly seeing what it would look like in a changed position is often hard to do. There is a need for the individual to gain recognition of patterns which become bits of knowledge that are then organised into larger and more meaningful units.

It is often the recognition of patterns that causes difficulties in the individual with DCD. The handling of spatial and temporal relationships may be the cause of the difficulties or with integration, sequencing or memory. The language complexity is also becoming greater at this stage and results in the adolescent often finding subjects like trigonometry and algebra a complete mystery.

Use of particular tools in mathematics such as a compass and a protractor may also be harder because of fine-motor difficulties. Trying to hold the paper and protractor at the same time may be difficult to manipulate. Too much pressure may be applied to compensate and end up with a hole in the paper. The individual may also have difficulties seeing objects being rotated in mathematics without actually physically moving them around.

- Using IT software packages to help the individual understand mathematics problems can be a great help. (Iansyst, AVP and REM all have a selection of programmes in the UK.)

- Creating 3D models may be necessary to explain concepts and build up a picture in the mind of the individual. This reinforces learning through both visual and kinaesthetic routes.

- Adaptation of some tools may also be needed such as Circle Scribe (instead of a protractor) or having a ruler with a handle on it, and Dycem (non-stick matting) to help keep the ruler in place when placed on the paper.

- Some adolescents may need to give commands to a learning support assistant to draw the objects that he wishes to display and may require this support in class.

- Use of an amanuensis in examinations requires practice in order for the individual to give the appropriate commands to be understood.

- Try to teach the individual the 'common language' and rules of mathematics (e.g. *add, addition, plus, and* for +).

The school environment

There are many areas in the school environment or about the school day that can cause difficulties for the individual. Knowing where the hotspots are helps to minimise difficulties. Many of the difficulties require time to gain the skills rather than intensive input.

Larger school

This can be bewildering. The young person with DCD often has a poor sense of direction and will get lost in a new environment. He may not recognise the blank walls, and the different buildings may look all the same. He has to negotiate from one site to another in quicker time as well as carrying all his possessions around.

- Maps of the school with indications on them of where they are situated can be helpful to all pupils as well as new staff members (like a shopping centre – 'you are here now').

Larger class size

This can leave the individual lost at the back of the class. Many young-sters will either adopt a 'class clown' approach or withdraw and be for-gotten as they make little attempt to interact in the class. If the youngster does try to do so and ask for help and the information is repeated, this may be viewed as lazy and inattentive, and not picked up as a sign that he may not have fully understood.

- Encouraging the individual to make sure that he has understood what he needs to do is important for the class teacher.

- Encouraging the individual to feel able to ask questions could be offered in class time, or an alternative arrangement made if possible afterwards, so as not to further highlight his difficulties.

- Information may need to be written down as well as orally given – could this be available for all the class so that the individual isn't again highlighted as THE one with difficulties?

- Consider which classes the individual is most inattentive in – is this because he or she has not fully understood the lesson and has become distractible because of boredom, or frustration?

- Check understanding – as the student may have got used to saying 'yes' when asked, to cover up his difficulties.

No desks or lockers

Some youngsters will be required to carry their possessions and books around with them all day. For those with DCD it can be extremely difficult to organise books and papers and not lose equipment on a very regular basis. He may compensate by carrying everything with him everywhere like a tortoise with his shell on his back. This can result in it being even harder for him to organise his work as well as having to carry around a very heavy load on his back. This may even cause the individual to develop back pain as he carries it in awkward position.

Folders and papers may become scrunched up at the bottom of the bag, making it harder at the end of the day to sort out where notes are supposed to be filed.

If there are lockers in use, they may have small and fiddly keys to deal with. This may make opening and closing them at speed between lessons harder to do. In addition he may end up losing key after key. Others may take this as not caring rather than seeing the severe organisational difficulties that may be occurring.

- Give consideration to where lockers are allocated – the end of a row may be easier.

- The option of having two lockers if the school is very large may help the pupil have dumping grounds to leave some books – the downside of this is he may become confused where he has left his belongings.

- Spare keys if they are lost or forgotten are also essential.

- Understand the reason for losing keys – this is not usually intentional as the individual makes very little gain out of this situation.

- Consider the type of bag used to carry books and the individual's posture – an over-the-shoulder bag can throw the posture out, as can a bag with insufficient support.

- Bags should always be worn on both shoulders with the back panel in close contact with the spine for support and the padded curve resting on the top of the buttocks to spread the load.

Different subjects, different approaches, different people

Not every teacher in secondary school will have a knowledge of the young person's difficulties and may lack expertise and experience supporting individuals with DCD. This has an impact on how the delivery of lessons needs to be adapted to allow the youngster to access the curriculum. Different approaches may be needed for different styles of subjects and topic areas e.g. history vs. chemistry.

- Risk assessment may be needed e.g. in chemistry or home economics. The adolescent may need to stand to do a task rather than sit to gain greater stability.

- He or she may require specific tools, such as with rubber handles, spreading tools or angle boards.

- Repetitive tasks such as chopping or fine-motor tasks such as accurate pouring may be harder to do, especially if there is a time constraint for the individual. Extra time may be needed to be built in or support given for parts of the task.

- He or she may need to work in a pair or in a three for practical tasks – one doing, and another recording, and the third observing. This also helps the individual to improve skills in social interaction, sharing and working as a part of a team.

- Transfer of information from one teacher to another is essential to ensure that understanding of the individual's learning styles and successful ways of working are shared so success is maximised.

The animal school

Once upon a time, the animals decided they must do something decisive to meet the increasing complexity of their society. They held a meeting and finally decided to organise a school. The curriculum consisted of running, climbing, swimming and flying. Since these were the basic behaviours of most animals they decided that all the students should take all the subjects.

The duck proved to be excellent at swimming, better, in fact, than his teacher. He also did well in flying. But he proved to be very poor in running. Since he was poor in this subject he was made to stay after school to practise it, and even had to drop swimming to get more time to practise running. He was kept at his poorest subject until his webbed feet were so badly damaged he became only average at swimming. But, average was acceptable in the school and nobody worried about that…except the duck.

The rabbit started at the top of his class in running, but finally had a nervous breakdown because of so much makeup time in swimming…a subject he hated.

The squirrel was excellent in climbing until he developed psychological blocking in flying class, where the teacher insisted he start flying from the ground instead of the tops of trees. He was kept at attempting to fly until he became muscle-bound and received a 'C' in climbing and a 'D' in running.

The eagle was the school's worst discipline problem. In climbing class he beat all of the others to the top of the tree, but he insisted on using his own method of getting there. He received an 'F'.

The gophers stayed out of school and fought the tax levies for education because digging was not included in the curriculum. They apprenticed their children to the badger and later joined the ground hogs to start a private school offering alternative education.

So the animals held another meeting and criticised the failure of the educational system to produce successful members of society.

Adapted by Amanda Kirby from *The Animal School*, by George H. Reavis (1999).

The animal school is a metaphor which reflects on the different types of learners in any environment. For the adolescent with DCD to flourish, he needs to develop a clear understanding of his strengths. At the same time the school needs to offer a variety of routes for the adolescent to be able to reach his goal.

The child with DCD may be weak at rugby but may be a good swimmer. However if swimming is not on offer then there are no opportunities for the individual to shine. The child with DCD may have great skills working with animals but there may be no opportunity to show this ability to empathise or take responsibility for caring for others.

Independent travel

The youngster may now need to travel to school independently and negotiate crossings, public transport, and have to manage money; all increasing the stress levels prior to arriving at school each day.

- Use of a bus pass may be helpful.

- Going to school accompanied, may be first necessary to practise on a new route and to gain confidence.

- Telling the adolescent where there are visual markers such as churches, garages, etc. to remind him where to get on or off a bus will be of help.

Homework

This may be the first time that the adolescent has additional work set at the end of the day. Catch-up and reading of notes may also be required. Note taking may be less legible and be incomplete if recording speeds are slower than his peers. For most young people with DCD, fatigue is something they live with. Each day requires a huge effort to concentrate and produce work. By the end of the day the adolescent is usually exhausted and often less able to be productive. He may also have not been able successfully to record all the homework, as the class may have been noisy and made it harder for him to hear as well as write the information down at speed. The combination of a noisy classroom, stress with regard to getting home or to another class, difficulty with recording, and disorganisation, make this one of the most stressful parts of the day and can lead to the individual ending up having a detention for failed work.

Other associated difficulties:

- He may alternatively believe that he has recorded the correct information but has missed out crucial information.

- He may have put the wrong books in his bag in error.

- Past experiences of difficulties with homework may increase the adolescent's anxiety when he arrives home, knowing that the next day he may get into trouble for failing to do his homework. This may make it hard for the individual even to sit down to start.

- His bag may be disorganised, making it hard for him to find relevant papers if they have been given out in class.

- Having the right tools for the job may be difficult as he may lose pencils, protractors, etc.

As a parent, facing the homework battle can mean ringing around every evening trying to find out what the homework *really* is. This is harder to do for the adolescent who may also be socially isolated as he may not have a large network of buddies he can readily ring to ask for the information.

- Giving homework on photocopied sheets will help to allow the adolescent to listen to instructions and not worry about recording it all at speed and in a legible form.

- A buddy network with phone numbers recorded to ring to check the homework if unsure, will also be helpful.

- A parent or classroom assistant to help organise the school bag will help the individual to 'see' what he has got to do and make sure the correct books get into the bag.

- A spare pencil case left at home and one kept in the school bag will mean the right tools can be found easily all the time.

- Essay templates and use of study techniques can help provide a framework for homework.

- A rest for the child when he comes home so that he has time to 'come to' before starting his work often helps.

- A regular timed start using a timer and buzzer system helps the individual know when work will start and mentally prepare for it.

- Colour-coded disks can be used to save work from the computer – placed in a disk holder to keep them together, or the computer set up with clearly marked folders to 'save' work into once completed.

Time concepts

The inner clock does not always seem to tick in the same way for the young person with DCD. He may not seem to be aware of time passing. However at the adolescent stage it becomes vital that he gains an understanding of the meaning of time, as he now has to, for example, complete examinations, be able to plan and organise his time appropriately, or be aware of when he is halfway through a test. This becomes a big problem for many secondary school children with DCD and remains so for many into adulthood.

- The youngster with DCD needs an external reminder of the time such as using alarms and buzzers to build up a 'feeling' of time.

- Alternatively, use regular trips and occasions as a measure for time, e.g. the 20-minute car journey to school each day, 10-minute walk to the local shops, 5 minutes reading in the evening.

- Use of a watch with pre-set alarms can also be helpful.

- Use of an egg timer to 'see' time passing.

The more routine activities are, the less effort they become; this helps to improve time management – see what elements of the day are repeated and create a routine that frees the adolescent to concentrate on the variables in his day.

Organisational skills

This is a key problem as the youngster is now supposed to be a more independent learner. He needs to plan and organise the writing of essays. He also needs to organise his work so that he can find what he wants at a later date. These skills are usually particularly weak.

- *Locker key* If the child has to have a locker key put it on a string or key ring or attach to trouser waist belt. It is helpful to make sure that there is a spare locker key at the school office.

- *Dress* Consider dress codes and ensure the child is not being penalised unfairly, e.g. tying his tie properly – could he be helped by having a Velcro tie concealed at the back?

- *Fasteners* Use of Velcro on clothes and elastic shoe laces in brown and black will help to speed up the process of changing for games, but is still discreet.

- *School rules* Consider school rules, are they implied or explicit? Could they be given to the individual written down and then also ensure that he or she has understood them? Is he also able to observe the implied ones – he may need help here.

- *Organising school bags* Could the individual be given some help to organise his bag and have poly-pockets (different colours) in A4 folders to separate notes into subjects. This may prevent everything being scrunched at the bottom of the bag!

- *Colour-coding disks* When used with PCs, these help the individual to remember that green is for geography, blue for science, etc., each subject having a different colour.

- *Audio tapes* Use of labelled and coded audio tapes for recording lessons is another alternative.

- *Laptops* Use of laptops will help to take the strain off the adolescent trying to record at speed. There is often a great emphasis played on learning to use the keyboard with accurate finger positions. However for the adolescent with DCD, this can act as an additional barrier. It is far better for the individual to have a go on the keyboard and be allowed to develop his own finger positions to suit him, rather than worrying where they are placed and resulting in him being put off using the keyboard at all. Fast speeds can be obtained by practice and encouraging use in the classroom to record will increase the speed.

- *Printer* Make sure that the individual has access to a printer in the school day and also can plug in his computer to charge if possible.

- *Copies* Carbon copying work or photocopying worksheets to minimise the need to record will mean the individual has an opportunity to listen and take in information and not record notes he would not be able to read later.

- *Pens* Use of roller ball instead of ink pen should be considered if this improves the quality of recording. A choice of implements is useful as everyone has different shape hands and different styles of pen grips. Use a talking pen recorder. A coloured pen could be used for mind mapping.

- *Mobile Phone* Can be used to organise homework or assignments.

- *Filofax* Diary to organise notes, dates and any other information.

- *Pencil cases* Use of see-through pencil case to see all contents and to have a list stapled to the inside.

- *Ruler* With a handle or ridge or a 'roller ruler' makes it easier to hold onto the ruler and stop it slipping when drawing.

- *Use a 'to-do list'* to start the day or before starting a piece of work so that a plan has been made and can be ticked off as the individual completes a task.

- *Use a timer* For all tasks so that the individual can build up a concept of time e.g. studying, etc.

- *Extra copies of timetables* These help to remind the adolescent what tasks need to be completed and prepare his bag accordingly for the following day.

- *Angled board* Upturned to improve posture.

Additional advice in sports:

- Consider non team based sports such as badminton, table tennis, fencing, swimming, trampolining. Co-ordination competence comes from practice.

- Offer ball skills training to build up skills – away from the main lesson.

- Allow an option for extra time for changing before and after the class if the individual is slower.

- Let the teacher choose the teams rather than the pupils so that the individual is not highlighted every week as the last to be chosen for the team.

- If a new game is being taught then it may be necessary to break it down into smaller components to learn the rules and how to play. Show how these components join together to form the basis for the game. It is important that the adolescent has a vision of what he needs to achieve.

- Consider that the child with movement and listening difficulties will find hearing instructions while trying to run across a field very difficult and will lose skills in one domain, either running or throwing e.g. in rugby or hockey.

Lunch

In most schools today this is canteen-style rather than a formal lunch setting. This may require the youngster to negotiate his lunch meal on a tray with a cup placed on it full of liquid passing others and manoeuvering around tables. This is difficult to do for most of us at the best of times, but is made much worse when others are jostling for position and balance and co-ordination are difficult even in a static position. He may alternatively choose something less nutritious but easier to handle and quicker to eat. However, opening a bag of crisps or even putting a straw in a carton may be difficult tasks for him.

- A balanced nutritional intake is essential for the individual with DCD, appropriate options should be sought to ensure that the adolescent eats well so that he or she does not resort to high-calorie/poorly nutritious options and additionally exacerbate weight gain.

- A snack sandwich and a drink packed in his bag may at least ensure that he has some food during the day – crisps ready opened and a sports cup with a built in straw may be options.

- Has he the right change for the school canteen? Make sure that this is sorted before school, so he is not left standing in a line while others are waiting for him.

Preparing for statutory examinations

Examinations put greater pressure on the adolescent, from both his family and his school. There is now an external measure of success or failure that may act to reinforce an already fragile self-esteem. The adolescent may feel that his output never quite matches what he understands and feels he is capable of achieving. This can be frustrating.

- Examination support and special provision needs to be assessed early to apply for additional arrangements. The individual needs to learn how to use this extra provision appropriately.

- Use of an amanuensis requires practice and shouldn't be introduced on the morning of the examinations – dictating and listening skills need to be shown to both the amanuensis and the student.

- Some children just require time prompts to allow them to reinforce how much time has passed.

- Extra time is not always the answer – some children may need to be examined in another room away from external noises and visual distractions.

- Exam planning is essential, so that if anxiety is heightened the individual has a template to start off the work.

Strategies for revising for examinations

Individuals with DCD may have difficulty working under time pressures and find that they work better with assignment-based courses. However, most individuals will still have a need to sit examinations in the early years and so may need some strategies to increase success rates.

- If the individual has already experienced success in exams, remember past strategies and continue to use them!

- Exam revision should be an element of your weekly work schedule throughout each term or semester. It is helpful to allocate at least one hour in the week for looking over notes and textbooks.

- Revise with a purpose, looking for the main concepts/principles/theories/facts/processes to do with the topic area. Sometimes this will involve memorisation (e.g. formulas, definitions, etc.), at other times it will mean identifying several major points.

- Work with a study partner if this is a way to reinforce your learning.

- Build a set of study notes drawn from lectures or talks and from text books. Some people make up a set of flash cards from their notes with a question on one side and the answer on the other.

Exam skills can be learned but usually need to be practised.

Making a revision timetable

- **What** has to be revised? – List each topic in every subject.
- **When** are the exams?
- Put one tick beside the topics that are **known well**, two ticks beside those that are **known less well**, and three ticks beside the topics that are not **known well at all** – cross the ticks out as topics are learned.
- **Estimate** the amount of time needed for each topic.
- Take a **monthly calendar** and mark in **when the exams are**. Add in other commitments.
- Draw up a **week-by-week** timetable with detailed **revision** sessions, **topic by topic**.
- Build in spare time, **'flexitime'**, when catch-up can occur or can be used as extra free time!
- **Know everything** about the exam – **when, where, how long, number and type of questions** (and whether they are compulsory or if there is a choice of questions).
- Leave time for **relaxation**, and normal school work and other commitments.

Find out exactly what is required for the test/exam and what is being tested.

- What will be covered and what will be omitted (refer to course outline)?
- List the things that need to be known and rank them in order of importance.
- Know what types of questions to expect (essay, short-answer, or multiple-choice, etc.).

- Find out how many questions, total time, and how marks are distributed over the questions.

- Check equipment needed, e.g. special pencils, calculator, or texts for open book exams.

- Get copies of previous exams if possible.

- Allocate study time in proportion to how much the test/exam counts towards the final grade.

Checklists

Equipment

- Pens, pencils, colours, rulers, maths equipment are with the individual before he leaves the house.
- Any **texts** that are allowed such as a dictionary.
- **Lucky mascot** if wanted.
- Make sure the individual is wearing a watch and it works and is accurate.

Night before

- Don't revise late.
- Don't try to learn new material.
- Check through (skim/scan) notes/typical questions.
- Relax before going to bed.
- Avoid others who are 'panic people'.

On the day

- Check where to go.
- Get up early enough to wake up.
- Eat sensibly – don't go to an exam without eating breakfast first and taking sandwiches/pasta for lunch.
- Arrive in good time: too early and others may increase panic; exactly on time can feel too late; five minutes before is about right.
- Have a bottle of water with you.

In the exam room

- Listen carefully to all the advice the teacher/tutor gives.
- Listen carefully to what the exam invigilator is saying.
- Check that all pages, questions, answer sheets, scrap paper, etc. are present.
- Read ALL the instructions on the paper...because they *can* change.
- Check the desk/chair is comfortable.
- Put the watch in a place where it can be seen.
- Check to ensure that the invigilator knows if extra time is being given.

Doing the exam

- Read the questions two to three times.
- Highlight (if it is allowed) key words in the questions.
- Determine how many questions and what kinds.
- Consider the weighting of marks each question carries.
- Estimate how long each part will take to finish.
- Expect to work quickly if there are many questions.
- Allow time for choosing, planning, and writing, checking and proofreading for essays, rather than launching in and not being able to have time at the end to correct any mistakes.
- CHECK THE TIME AFTER EACH PART IS COMPLETED.
- If there is a shortage of time, write an introduction, outline the argument in note form, and then write the conclusion.

Advice on special arrangements for external examinations

1. Consider and plan early if you think special arrangements may need to be made.

2. Each examination has to be applied for – there are almost always no 'blanket' special arrangements.

3. Time allowances will vary depending on the type of examination and the difficulty faced by the individual – 25 per cent is usually the most that will be offered.

4. If the individual has a Statement of Special Educational Needs, it does not mean he will automatically have special arrangements made – the child may need an up-to-date literacy assessment or a relevant diagnostic report by an educational psychologist or appropriately qualified teacher – this usually needs to have been completed within the last two years.

5. English language – extra time can be given and rest periods, but it is highly unlikely that an amanuensis will be allowed. An amanuensis is a person who writes down, types or word processes a candidate's dictated answers to questions.

6. Individuals should have practice and experience of the special arrangements requested.

7. The individuals can have special arrangements where reading or writing is a difficulty.

8. Supervised rest periods can be given, which will not be taken off the examination time.

9. Separate invigilation can be given if appropriate with a reader, or the candidate can be allowed to sit the examination in a separate room and read the questions out loud.

10. Prompters are occasionally allowed to tell the candidate that time is passing at particular points. A prompter is usually used where there are attentional difficulties, e.g. to give a light tap on the candidate's arm or desk to prompt them back on the task – verbal prompts are not allowed.

11. Word processors without spell checks can be allowed in examinations.

12. The paper may be allowed to be re-written if it is not sufficiently legible. However this is unusual as most individuals would have an amanuensis arranged rather than a re-written transcript.

13. Extra time may be based on writing or reading speed, where diagrams are required or turning pages is difficult, or for completion of practical tasks.

14. Enlarged grids for mathematics and other technical subjects can be supplied where filling these in is a problem, or an amanuensis may be permitted for drawing and labelling lines, etc.

Other techniques for studying

Visual mapping (also known as spidergrams and mind maps) is a mechanism to plan and record information using visual tags and maps. There are also electronic versions available to use on computers as well, such as Mind Manager and Inspiration. With any new technique there requires a period of practising a skill, which may seem to slow the student down. Practise at times where there is less pressure. A new simple 'post-it' note program called 'StickUp' can be used to start off this process and can be easily learned.

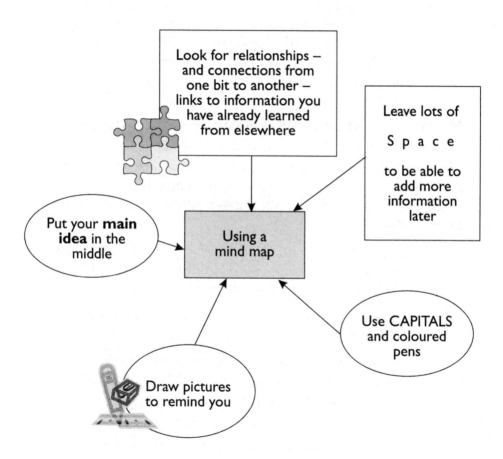

Figure 8.1 Using a mind map

Bomb blasting is a technique that uses post-it notes to 'throw' down ideas and move them around until they 'look' right. There are '**post-it note**' programs that can be downloaded from the computer and also commercially available ones that can sit on the computer and aid organisation and planning.

- Use a highlighter pen to make the important facts stand out.

- Write brief notes on to **post cards** or index cards to minimise information – a useful technique for last-minute studying.

- '**Record and scrunch**' – scribble it down and then throw it out – helps if the process of writing helps to remember the topic. This is especially true for the kinaesthetic learner who learns better doing a task rather than listening how to do a task.

Making career choices and planning for further education

For many teenagers, making an appropriate career choice is hard enough. Those with DCD may not yet have an awareness of their strengths at all and only see the difficulties. Executive dysfunction may lead to the adolescent not being able to assess the situation fully and make appropriate and wise choices.

- Careers advice may need to be planned in small steps to show the adolescent how he or she may reach the goal set and what skills he will need to acquire in order to succeed.

- The individual may need to access local careers services for an in-depth skills profiling.

- Short-term and long-term goal setting is a good start to building up a profile of where the individual sees himself in the next few months and years.

- Learning needs and preferences should be delineated; these are useful to inform others when moving from one learning environment to another.

- There is also a need to plan for each transition process.

The following questions need to be considered:

- Where will the adolescent study once he or she leaves school?

- What support will be needed? Can he or she apply for a disability students' allowance?

- Which colleges or universities understand the needs of the young adult with DCD?

- Where should the individual study – in the individual's home town, where there will be continuing parental support and more familiar surroundings, or further afield?

- If a decision to move away is taken, then how far should that be – what transport is available to get home easily if this is required?

- Where should the individual live – in a hall of residence or in a flat? Has he or she the necessary independent living skills if trying to cope on his or her own?

The following template is provided to show what changes may need to be considered – by either the individual or by changing the school environment – in order to give appropriate support.

(This may also be photocopied as a teaching resource or used to highlight where support is required and be used as a checklist in helping to construct key elements of the Individual Education Plan.)

Difficulty	Changing the individual	Changing the environment
Examinations – finish in time		
Writing		
Class notes		
Essays/ Assignments		
Homework		
Science lessons		
Mathematics		
P.E.		
Cookery/CDT		
Disorganised		
Poor time management		

This chart has been filled in to give specific practical guidance in the different areas of difficulty that may affect the adolescent with DCD.

Difficulty	Changing the individual	Changing the environment
Examinations – finish in time	Wearing a watch with a pre-set alarm.	Extra time. Being told when extra time starts, clock in room easily visible. Prompting during the examination.
Writing	Gaining keyboard skills. Trial of different writing implements to see if this aids writing.	Amanuensis or use of laptop for examinations and in classroom setting. Appropriate desk and chair so that the individual is in a stable position.
Class notes	Learning to mind map/use mind mapping software.	Provision of tape recorder to record lessons. Lesson plan given so that student sees outline and aims. Notes from class photocopied. Carbon copy of students' notes. Notes only requiring 'gaps' to be filled in.
Essays/ Assignments	Learn how to use templates, power point, IT software to help plan and organise thoughts onto paper.	Provide template. Teach study skills. Provide IT options to try out. Alternative MCQ testing. (multiple choice questionnaire)

Homework	Homework diary to record all work to be completed. Mini voice recorder to record short information – attached to personal belongings. Homework buddy with home telephone number so call up can be arranged if necessary.	Continue to record homework and check correct books put into bag. Colour code homework planner. Timetable to plan ahead when homework needs to be given in. Homework posted on school intranet to access at a later stage.
Science lessons	Work in a group.	Allow to observe rather than carry out experiments. Do a 'Risk Assessment' for equipment and position. Allow the child to stand rather than sit. Provide adapted tools.
Mathematics	Understanding abstract concepts – there is a need to use kinaesthetic and visual methods.	Introduce IT and visual programs such as specific maths programs like 'Numicon'. Use 3D cut outs to explain 2D problems to allow the student to see visually and kinaesthetically the concepts. Check on language comprehension of key mathematical terms – e.g. *on, under, into, division.*
P.E.	Ensure clothes are adapted if necessary so that the individual can make a quick change.	Look at basic ball skills. Build up shoulder and hip stability – use exercises that the whole class can do. Work on stamina training. Be aware that understanding direction and moving may be harder to do.

Cookery/CDT	Encourage student to risk assess and plan preparation.	Make sure the tools are appropriate. e.g. use Dycem under bowls and rubber handled knives, butter board for spreading. Have recipes photocopied to follow and tick off.
Disorganised	'To-do' lists. Use voice recorder. Use a see-through pencil case with list attached to the inside. Repetition of new skills to become automatic.	Mentor or buddy to help organise. Assistance from LSA with planning and organising self and workplace. Help with colour-coding of files, poly-pockets for notes, colour-coded disks for computer. Use of goal planning and review to give students skills. Regular meetings through the work for short periods to consider forward planning and allow the student to establish working patterns.
Poor time management	Watch with buzzer alarm. Timers. Planners for everyday and for homework.	To understand time concepts – predicting time requirements for assignments. To build up a realistic plan.

Case study

George is 12 years old. He has had to stay behind after school as he has persistently not been giving in work in geography for the past few weeks. George always seems to bring the wrong books along to the class.

In considering what is happening here, it is necessary to look at George's whole timetable. The lesson before geography one day a week is preceeded by P.E.. George has to change from his kit back into uniform and then get from one end of the school to the other. P.E. has never been very good for George, who gets confused if he hears a long string of instructions and is not as fast as the others. He is slow changing and always arrives at geography in a fluster. He finds drawing maps in geography impossible. The other kids even laugh at his attempts sometimes!

The geography teacher, George says, dictates most of the lesson notes to the class rather than writing them down. He has lost his textbook and has to lean over to look at the boy's next to him. George is a bit 'floppy' and tends to lean on the other boy until he gets fed up and moves his book over to the other side.

At the end of the lesson George has to listen to the homework and always finds he can't get it down quickly and can't ask again as he has to rush to another class at the other end of the school.

George doesn't have many friends. At the end of the day, he doesn't have anyone he can ring to ask for more detail on the homework, even though he wants to get it right.

What should be done for George?

It is so important to ensure that we see the whole picture rather than snippets before making judgements.

9 Moving On and Moving Out

Introduction

Personal care

Organising your studying at home

In the kitchen

Money management

Learning to drive a car

Be not afraid of growing slowly, be only afraid of standing still.

Ancient Chinese proverb

Most of the shadows of this life are caused by standing in one's own sunshine.

Ralph Waldo Emerson

Never measure the height of a mountain, until you have reached the top. Then you will see how low it was.

Daj Hammarskjold

Introduction

For most parents, being a successful parent means seeing your child leave home and move on to an independent life. For many adolescents, the first steps from the comfort, security and support from home to college or university can feel pretty nerve-racking. For the individual with DCD, this can be three times as hard. Finding your way around a new town or campus, making friends, organising your day are all areas that cause difficulty for the individual.

Preparation prior to going can make the difference between success and failure.

For individuals with DCD, there are always two routes, both ending at the same place. The first is the direct and more traditional one, but sometimes ends in failure; the second is finding the support required or a way around the obstacle to get to where he or she wants to be. This may seem to take longer, but the journey is more surely completed. Time is usually the greatest barrier and if extra time can be given then success will usually be seen.

For the parent, knowing how much to support and how much to pull back can be a real dilemma. There is no clear rule book – only some suggestions.

Personal care

The individual with DCD while still at home may have the support from his parents in helping to make clothing choices and to provide a constant stream of clean clothes in the cupboard. Once he has left home to move into his own accommodation or is in a hall of residence at university, this support has suddenly been removed.

Like many first-time students this can be a nasty wake up call. The individual with DCD in this respect is like many other students. However organising what needs to be cleaned and when may be a problem and may even require a rescue operation from his parents on a semi-regular basis to ensure that it does not become completely out of hand. (Black bags, bleach and rubber gloves may be a requirement for this operation!)

It may be useful before moving out to practise some of the skills that may be needed, such as using a washing machine (opening plastic packets of washing tablets may need a pair of scissors if this is a difficulty), using a coin-operated washing machine, learning to fold clothes rather than needing to iron them.

In addition setting up the room with appropriate tools for the job at the beginning of term can yield enormous dividends. The student may require a set of cleaning materials (make sure he can open the bottles to be used), a bag for dirty washing, a supply of coins for the launderette, sufficient hangers to hang clothes (strong ones as he may tend to end up piling clothes on one hanger only).

If the student has his own shower area in the university, it may be worth putting a rubber mat in the shower to minimise the risk of slipping. A towel with a cloth loop may also be useful to help the individual to hang it up after showering rather than falling to the floor.

Try providing socks that are all similar so pairing the socks together is less of an issue. A suitable electric shaving kit for boys is often easier to use than a wet shaver. For girls, dividers for drawers to separate underwear as well as using dividers to organise makeup may be useful.

Try and see if a style of dress can be established before going to university. A sibling or family friend is the ideal person to do this. A parent's style is never quite the right thing for a good student image. Once this has been done, the student will probably wear similar clothes most of the time and this will limit the need to worry about matching items. Now the student can chose his own clothing on a day-to-day basis, he can easily avoid difficult fastenings and only needs to wear slip-on shoes or trainers. Encourage the student before leaving to get into a washing routine for himself and his clothes. The more these tasks are automated the less effort is required and is therefore less stressful.

A shorter hairstyle for either boys or girls means that self-care can be minimised, especially when time is in short supply in the morning.

Organising your studying at home

In order to develop good organisational approaches to everyday tasks the adolescent needs to see a gain from the effort. Organising himself and his surroundings may take some time before these are automated actions. Change can sometimes seem like more work than leaving things as they are, and the status quo sometimes seems a better option.

Try not to introduce this list of ideas all at once. One new approach successfully taken on board and implemented may make a difference. Only introduce a second strategy when the first is fully embedded into everyday actions.

Start off the way you mean to continue – Go out with the individual and buy an organiser kit. This should contain the following:

- A corkboard (unless it is already provided) to place notices, timetables etc.

- In-trays to place work in some order before filing it.

- Dividers and coloured lever arch files – each subject should be colour coded to make it easier to file.

- Sticky labels to stick on the lever arch files so that each subject can be clearly seen at a glance for filing purposes.

- Poly-pockets – these plastic wallets are useful to place loose pieces of paper and to be put in the lever arch file.

- Folders for assignments – these are ready to ensure work looks presentable.

- Coloured floppy discs to colour code work saved from the computer.

- A disk box for both CDs and floppy disks so they are not left strewn all over the floor.

- A pen holder with a variety of writing implements.

- A supply of printer cartridges and a couple of reams of paper for printing, if a computer and printer are being used.

Consider planning the timetable at the start of the term – Once the timetable has been sorted out at college, it is worth sitting down with a parent or student support services to see when work needs to be completed and how the week flows. Support can then be sought for the times where there may be greater pressure on the individual.

Have a notebook, palm pilot or 'to-do' list handy – It is useful to be able to record things that need doing somewhere where they can be retrieved afterwards. Many mobile phones have an organiser function and are useful to minimise the number of bits of kit that need to be carried around. Have a running shopping list so that when the student goes out to shop he already has a reminder of what he has run out of.

Watch out for time – Time is one of the key problems for the student with DCD and a large clock will be easier to see and harder to lose. A mobile phone can be used as an alarm clock for getting up in the morning. Encourage the student to wear a watch – a waterproof one is best so that it can be worn all the time. A watch with alarms can then be preset as reminders at certain times during the day.

Checklist for studying		
	Yes	No
Post-it notes		
Pens, pencils, ruler, colours		
Highlighter pens		
Plastic wallets		
All types of paper		
Index cards/floppy disks for the computer		
Timetables and planners		
Calculator		
Cartridges and ink		
Corrector fluid		
Homework questions		
Dividers, files, hole punch		
Past exam papers		
Drink		
Text/reference books		

MONDAY TO FRIDAY PLANNER

Name:		Week Commencing:		
MONDAY	TUESDAY	WEDNESDAY	THURSDAY	FRIDAY

L U N C H

WEEKLY PLANNER

Name:	Week commencing:	

MONDAY	TUESDAY	WEDNESDAY	THURSDAY	FRIDAY	SATURDAY	SUNDAY

LUNCH

TO-DO LIST

Name: _____ Date: _____

	Tick when completed
1.	
2.	
3.	
4.	
5.	
6.	
7.	
8.	
9.	
10	
11.	
12.	

Special Attention:

In the kitchen

Preparing a meal and getting it on the table hot can be a challenge if there are major organisational difficulties. Problems can occur in deciding what to make, the order to prepare the meal, cutting and slicing and then combining the whole thing together and getting it on the table, so it isn't cold before attempting to eat it.

The difficulty may stem from trying to use an instrument in the kitchen such as an egg separator, balancing the tool and trying to crack the egg together requires good fine-motor co-ordination and timing. A range of tools can be used to aid the individual in the kitchen.

A checklist of suitable equipment

- An electric can opener – this leaves your hands free.
- Slicing bread on a fixed board – this holds the bread in place and makes it easier to slice.
- Cracking an egg – it may be difficult when trying to do this on the side of the bowl using one hand. Cracking too hard means the egg white, yolk and shell all end up in the bowl. By using an egg separator with a rest on it, the yolk can stay in one part while the white falls through to the bowl and increases the chances of being able to make a soufflé or meringues.
- Opening a jar – use a rubber gripper or a metal holder.
- Bread spreader – this fixes the bread in one place while spreading it.
- Tipper kettles – this stops it spilling everywhere.
- Plugs with handles – easier to pull in and out of the socket.
- Sieve with rests – frees hands to hold the spoon and the bowl.
- A timer in the kitchen is an essential piece of kit – setting it every time to know starting and finishing times.

- Fine chopping may require adapted tools such as rubber-handled knives or even electric food processors.

- Another difficulty may be following a recipe in the correct order. Missed items in a recipe may be a result of feeling under undue pressure to get tasks done in a certain time to ensure a complete hot meal is produced.

- Learning basic skills and a number of set recipes may mean the adolescent gains confidence in not only preparing meals for him or herself but for the whole family and friends and can act as a real boost to self-confidence.

- Photocopying recipes so that items can be crossed off as they have been added to the recipe may also be helpful – highlighting the instructions may make them easier to follow.

- Preparation of cold meals may be easier to start with as they are not so time-sensitive.

- The one-pot meal is the answer to balanced cooking arriving at the table hot.

- Resting the cookery book on a book rest may make it easier to use.

- A basic microwave may allow the individual to make simple snacks and the timer 'pinging' when it has finished is an additional auditory reminder.

- Spend time planning meals, it will save time when preparing for them. You can't make an omelette without eggs!

- Practise using different utensils at home when there is more time available.

- Check out handles of kitchen gadgets – there are some with rubber grips which are easier to hold.

- Make a personal recipe book – write out the individual recipes you can make, or just make notes of food you have eaten at other people's homes and ask them to write out the recipe. Tear out recipes from magazines. There is no need to stick to them exactly. Start with simple recipes and then adapt them. A pound of mince, onions and a tin of tomatoes can be turned into spaghetti bolognese, cottage pie, chilli, and lasagne quite easily, for example.

- Use convenience foods when entertaining if that helps.

- If in a rush choose sandwiches or finger food.

- Organise cupboards, label drawers to make it easy to find everything.

- Know where water/electricity can be switched off.

- Sit if your balance is compromised.

Use a menu planner to decide what is going to be made for the week, and what will need to be bought. This can be used to see if meals are balanced nutritionally as well. This can also help with budgeting, making sure there is enough money to last the week.

Weekly menu – example	
Monday	Chicken curry
Tuesday	Spaghetti with tomato sauce
Wednesday	Cheese and potato pie with baked beans
Thursday	Vegetable and bean casserole
Friday	Lamb chops and jacket potato
Saturday	Pizza and salad
Sunday	Roast chicken, potatoes and vegetables
Notes: Need to buy curry powder, pizza, garlic	

Some tips for preparing a meal:

- Plan the order of preparation – get out the necessary ingredients.

- Photocopy the page where the recipe is and tick the steps off as they are completed.

- Clear up as tasks are completed.

- Consider making a shopping list with two sides to it – one with the regular items you get every week and the other side with extras. This could be laminated so that items could be wiped off as new items are added each week. Alternatively have some photocopied sheets that can be taken when shopping.

Money management

This may be a difficulty, perhaps due to poorer organisational skills or an inability to do mathematical tasks when under pressure. Today there is less need to add up single items in a supermarket. Most of the time it is more useful to gain knowledge of a weekly basket of food, or single items such as CDs and computer programs.

- Using a season ticket on buses or trains reduces the need for sorting change when, for example, there is a queue of people behind you.

- Shopping online can be one way of taking time and checking purchase prices at a pace that is set by the individual rather than by others. This may take time to initially set up but allows the individual to do this at their own speed. Delivery to the door also means that packing and carrying several items is avoided.

- Having a bank account may teach the individual at this age to start to be able to manage his or her expenditure and could be reviewed on a monthly basis to start the process of learning about planning expenses and matching it with income.

- Pocket money for selected items also allows some of the budgeting skills to be practised.

If you are going to live independently you need to consider how you will manage your money. It can be hard to start to consider what bills will come in at the end of the month, when instead you want to go out and have a good time.

- Sit down with a pen and paper and write down all the bills expected to be received, e.g. telephone, electricity, gas, water and rates. If there is a car, road tax, as well as MOT, petrol and servicing, need to be considered. Put dates when they have to be paid.

- Is there a bank account where earnings and any other payments are paid into? If not, consider talking to the bank, there is usually someone there to help set up a budget account. This allows a certain amount to paid in each month automatically and spread out over the year. It prevents running out of money when the bills come in.

- By planning weekly meals and budgeting for them, it is easier for the individual to see how to make more economical meals and not blow all the money on, for example, pizzas and fish and chips. Convenience foods can sometimes be quite a bit more expensive.

Learning to drive a car

The young adult may find the thought of driving a car too great even to contemplate after years of having to struggle with anything with wheels. Learning to cope with gears while negotiating the road may feel very frightening.

Try to break the whole job of learning to drive into smaller tasks so that he or she can gain the skills in one area before moving on. Simulated lessons have an advantage of safety and ability to repeat skills training but at the present time they are only on manual cars in the UK.

The instructor needs to be told that he or she may need to repeat instructions and not to rush the adolescent through the lessons. It may take longer, but it doesn't mean he won't get there in the end.

An instructor who has worked with individuals with hearing impairments will describe the route using visual cues, which may help more than using right and left cues alone. For example, use of a marker such as buildings can help the student to know where to turn.

- Learning on a geared car may become too much of a challenge and may mean that using an automatic car becomes a preferred option. If the individual has perceptual difficulties, then tasks such as parking may be more difficult.

- Having a car with an auditory warning system is an ideal addition to avoid too many bumps.

- Encourage the learner driver to use mirrors for reversing, as his perception of depth and distance may not be very good. He may find he turns round to look and then takes his eyes off the road. One of the key difficulties for the driver with DCD is being able to do a series of tasks at once. He may be able to concentrate on the steering but then not concentrate on road safety. Off-road training to start with may be one way to gain some of the skills, rather than trying to learn them all at once.

- MAVIS (see Useful addresses) in the UK provides assessments for individuals that may require additional assistance. A patient teacher is essential.

- Practical suggestions include putting a red sticker on the right of the steering wheel to remind the user visually and quickly, right from left.

- Simulated lessons are available from some British School of Motoring centres for manual cars and may be a safer alternative before launching onto the roads. They can be started before the individual is 17 years of age.

- BSM have a 'MAP' CD-ROM program that can help the individual learn some of the skills required using a computer.

- Buying a driving computer game with a steering wheel and brakes can be a good way of practising steering and gaining control as well as learning to be aware of obstacles in the road!! A computer crash is always cheaper than a real one!

Case study

Getting support at university

Simon is 18 years of age and has just completed his A-levels and has a place at a university to do film studies and music production. He is excited at the prospect. However, his parents are concerned for his welfare as it will be the first time he has really left home for any length of time.

Simon tends to be disorganised and will often ring his mother up when out in the local town asking for a lift home as he has wandered off and got on the wrong train in the wrong direction.

He has been beaten up a couple of times when he has met the 'wrong' sort of person and they have taken advantage of his naivety and have taken money from him. Simon often does not spot the danger signs until it is too late.

His mother is deeply concerned for him but sees it is the time for him to go to university. She wants him to tell the college of his difficulties as soon as possible rather than wait till problems occur. Simon doesn't want her to come to the learning resource centre meeting with him. His mother wants to be able to tell them some of the problems he has had in the past as she does not see him doing this himself.

In the end they both decide that she will write a letter pointing the difficulties out and he can take that with him to the meeting. She will then meet the support team when she takes him to university.

Case study

Settling in to college

Janet is now 22 years of age and living with other girls in a house while studying photography at a local college. In the first term she was in total chaos and got into trouble for having assignments in late and missing lectures.

She finds it difficult to cope in the house if the other girls move objects and furniture around. She needed help when putting her computer together as she couldn't get it out of the box or put the parts together. She knew where they all went, but it was the dexterity required to put it together that she found so hard.

She took some advice regarding her organisation and now has a big corkboard in her room with her timetable, and baskets to throw her clothes in. The other girls now prompt her when she needs to leave so that she can get to college on time.

A learning support tutor meets with her once a week and goes through her timetable and work schedule and plans with her the assignments she needs to complete. She is feeling far less anxious now she has this level of support.

References

Gilger, J.W. and Kaplan, B.J. (2001) 'Atypical brain development: A conceptual framework for understanding developmental learning disabilities.' *Developmental Neuropsychology 20,* 465–481.

Kadesjo, B. and Gillberg, C. (1998) 'Attention deficits and clumsiness in Swedish 7-year-old children.' *Developmental Medicine and Child Neurology 40,* 796–804.

Kadesjo, B. and Gillberg, C. (2001) 'The comorbidity of ADHD in the general population of Swedish school-age children.' *Journal of Child Psychology and Psychiatry 42,* 487–492.

Kaplan, B.J. *et al.* (1998) 'DCD may not be a discrete disorder.' *Human Movement Science 17,* 4–5, 471.

Losse, A., Henderson, S.E., Elliman, D., Hall, Knight, E. and Jongmans, M. (1991) 'Clumsiness in children: Do they grow out of it? A 10-year follow up study.' *Developmental Medicine and Child Neurology 33,* 55–68.

Missiuna, C. (2001) *Children with Developmental Co-ordination Disorder: Strategies for Success.* Binghampton, NY: The Haworth Medical Press.

Skinner, R.A. and Piek, J.P. (2001) 'Psychosocial implications of poor motor coordination in children and adolescents.' *Human Movement Science 20,* 1–2, 73–94.

Stevenson, C.S., Whitmont, S., Bornholt, L., Livesey, D. and Stevenson, R.J. (2002) 'A cognitive remediation programme for adults with attention deficit hyperactivity disorder.' *Australia and New Zealand Journal of Psychiatry 36,* 5, 610–616.

Willoughby, C.P., Polatajko, H., Currado, C., Harris, K. and King, G. (2000) 'Measuring the self-esteem of adolescents with mental health problems: Theory meets practice.' *Canadian Journal of Occupational Therapy 67,* 4, 230–238.

Useful Additional Reading

Blackerby, D. (1996) *Rediscover the Joy of Learning.* Success Skills, Inc.

Bolick, T. (2001) *Asperger Syndrome and Adolescence: Helping Pre-teens and Teens Get Ready for the Real World.* Fair Winds.

Brown, D.S. (2000) *Learning a Living.* Woodbine House.

Bustamante, E.M. (2000) *Treating the Disruptive Adolescent: Finding the Real Self Behind Oppositional Defiant Disorders.* Jason Aronson.

Cermak, S. and Larkin, D. (2002) *Developmental Co-ordination Disorder.* Delmar.

Colley, M. and the Dyspraxia Foundation Adult Support Group (2000) *Living with Dyspraxia: A guide for Adults with Developmental Dyspraxia.* Dyspraxia Foundation.

Covey, S. (1998) *The 7 Habits of Highly Effective Teens.* Simon & Schuster.

Csóti, M. (1999) *People Skills for Young Adults.* Jessica Kingsley Publishers.

Kirby, A. and Drew, S. (2003) *Guide to Dyspraxia and Development Co-ordination Disorders.* David Fulton Publishers.

McKay, M. and Fanning, P. (2003) *Self-Esteem: A Proven Program of Cognitive Techniques for Assessing, Improving and Maintaining Your Self-Esteem.* New Harbinger Publishers.

Missiuna, C. (2001) *Children With Developmental Coordination Disorder: Strategies for Success.* Haworth Press.

Nortledge, A. (1990) *The Good Study Guide.* Open University Press.

Ripley, K. (2001) *Inclusion for Children with Dyspraxia: A Handbook for Teachers.* David Fulton Publishers.

Rae, T. (2000) *Confidence, Assertiveness and Self Esteem: For Secondary Pupils.* Lucky Duck.

Smith Myles, B. and Adreon, D. (2001) *Asperger Syndrome and Adolescence: Practical Solutions for School Success.* Jessica Kingsley Publishers.

Useful Addresses

The Dyscovery Centre
4a Church Road
Whitchurch
Cardiff CF14 2DZ
Tel: 029 2062 8222
Fax: 029 2062 8333
E-mail: dyscoverycentre@btclick.com
Website: www.dyscovery.co.uk

The Dyscovery Trust
4a Church Road
Whitchurch
Cardiff CF14 2DZ
Tel: 029 2061 5620
Website: www.dyscoverytrust.org.uk

The Dyspraxia Foundation
West Alley
Hitchin
Hertfordshire SG5 IEG
Tel: 01462 454986
E-mail: dyspraxia@dyspraxiafoundation.org.uk
Website: www.dyspraxiafoundation.org.uk

Dyspraxia Association of Ireland
c/o 389 Ryevale Lawns Leixlip
Co Kildare
Ireland
E-mail: dyspraxiaireland@eircom.net

DANDA (Development Adult Neurodiversity Association)
46 Westbere Road
London NW2 3RU
Tel: 020 7435 7891

MAVIS (Mobility Advice and Vehicle Information Service)
Macadam Avenue
Old Wokingham Road
Crowthorne
Berkshire RG45 6XD
Tel: 01344 661000
Fax: 01344 661066
E-mail: mavis@dft.gsi.gov.uk
Website: www.dft.gov.uk

Subject Index

Name Index

American Psychiatric Association 17
AVP 91

Bornholt, L. 60

Circle Scribe 91
Currado, C. 60

DANDA (Development Adult Neurodiversity Association) 9, 137
DSM-lV criteria 17, 18
Dycem 91
Dyscovery Centre (The) 136
Dyscovery Trust (The) 136
Dyspraxia Association of Ireland 136
Dyspraxia Foundation (The) 9, 136

Elliman, D. 14

Gilger, J.W. 14
Gillberg, C. 13, 15, 55

Hall 14
Harris, K. 60
Henderson, S.E. 14

Iansyst 91

Individual Learning/Education Plan (ILP/IEP) 82, 88
Inspiration 109

Jongmans, M. 14

Kadesjo, B. 13
Kaplan, B.J. 14
King, G. 60
Knight, E. 14

Livesey, D. 60
Loss, A. 14

'MAP' (CD-ROM) 130
MAVIS (Mobility Advice and Vehicle Information Service) 130
Mind Manager 109
'Mindreading' 63

Piek, J.P. 16
Polatajko, H. 60

REM 91

Skinner, R.A. 16
Statement of Special Educational Needs 107-108
Stevenson, C.S. 60
Stevenson, R.J. 60
'StickUp' computer program 27, 28

Whitmont, S. 60
Willoughby, C.P. 60
World Health Organisation 17